NATIONAL DEBUT

Her 1969 Wellesley College commencement address won her a seven-minute standing ovation—and a spot in *Life* magazine. "Good expressions and hand gestures," the photographer said of the shoot, at Hillary's home in Park Ridge, Illinois. "Her glasses helped."

TIME

HILLARY
AN AMERICAN LIFE

NEW HAMPSHIRE REBOUND
Hillary (greeting predawn voters in Manchester with Chelsea in 2008) won big after a third-place finish in Iowa.

CAMERA READY *Presidential primary candidate Clinton walks a Las Vegas neighborhood in 2008 with popular assemblyman Ruben Kihuen (left).*

CONTENTS

4 The Undaunted One
By Michael Scherer

8 Can Anyone Stop Her?
By David Von Drehle

20 By the Numbers

22 Evolution of a Leader By Alex Altman

38 White House Lessons
By Michael Crowley

54 The Senate Overachiever
By Zeke Miller

64 A First Bid for President
By Jay Newton-Small

76 Circling a Troubled Globe
By Massimo Calabresi

90 The TIME Covers

92 Anchored by Faith
By Elizabeth Dias

100 The Family Business By Haley Sweetland Edwards

Portions of this book were previously published in TIME magazine.

Just a couple of weeks after arriving at the White House in 1993, Hillary Rodham Clinton was already telling confidants she could not stand her new city. >

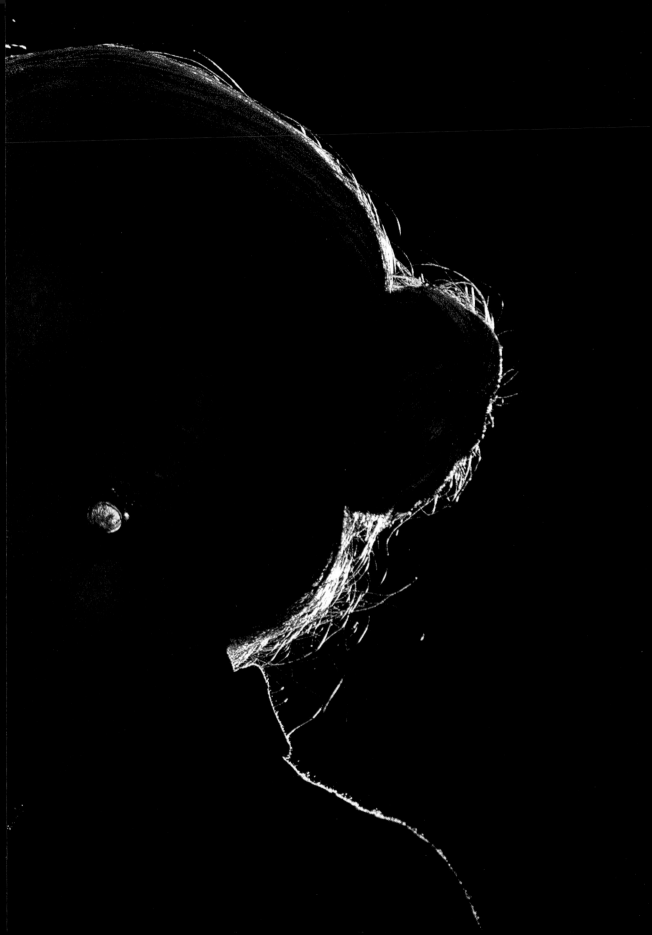

Her best friend, Diane Blair, described the First Lady's views at the time: "baffled and angered by D.C. attitude and ways," Blair wrote of her friend in her diary that year. It turned out to be an understatement.

In the years that followed, through scandals, policy and personal disasters and Bill Clinton's impeachment, Blair's diary cataloged Clinton's many complaints. The First Lady was "dumbfounded" by the people who lied to her. She described U.S. senators as "diseased from egomania." She joked that she had been bonding with creeps and knocked the press as "complete hypocrites." It was a seemingly endless lament, but its most remarkable features lay elsewhere—never did Clinton's vexation turn to hopelessness, and there is little evidence that she ever seriously reconsidered her calling to public life. As the hits kept coming, she bore down and kept going.

This much can be said of Hillary Clinton as she approaches the next chapter in her life: the daughter of a Chicago textile salesman, the first student commencement speaker in Wellesley College history, the former First Lady who went on to become a U.S. senator from New York, a U.S. secretary of state and the most admired woman in America, as measured by Gallup for 17 of the past 20 years, is not one to let obstacles overcome her. Instead, time and again, stresses, failures and humiliations seem to have a vivifying effect on par with her successes. She relishes the trials and seeks out more. "I can't stand whining," she declared in a 2012 interview with *Marie Claire* magazine, just a few months before leaving her most recent job running the State Department. "I can't stand the kind of paralysis that some people fall into because they're not happy with choices they made." In the days after her husband's impeachment for lying about his affair with a White House intern, Clinton was even blunter in a private conversation with her friend. "Most people in this town have no pain threshold," Blair recorded her saying.

This quality may soon be revealed as the key to unlocking the great mystery that has enveloped Hillary Clinton in her new life, without official title. Her biography on Twitter now ends with a tease: "hair icon, pantsuit aficionado, glass ceiling cracker, TBD..." The last part—shorthand for "to be determined" followed by tantalizing ellipses—looks increasingly like a second run at the White House. Her friends are already organizing on her behalf, and her own schedule vibrates with unflagging ambition. Rather than relaxing at the age of 66, she has been zipping around the country reconnecting with political allies, getting photographed with an expanding network of political donors, sending handwritten notes to old friends and publishing yet another political memoir, which promises yet another book tour after the midterm elections. She claims that no decision has been made on a run, even though every move she makes suggests one.

The Democratic Party, meanwhile, which revolted in the face of her aura of inevitability during the 2008 campaign, has all the marks of entrancement. No one in her party has yet stepped in. She seems to have earned the place at the table she always believed she deserved, and there are signs that she has been studying the mistakes of her last run. In early 2014, her public polls were near their historical highs, with close to 70% of the country calling her "likable" in a CNN poll and 64% saying she is tough enough to handle a crisis, a full 11 points ahead of President Obama in the same poll. On paper, she is tantalizingly close to lording over the city she long ago came to despise.

But she also knows more than most just how costly it is to remain in the public eye.

RESTED AND READY? *Hillary (here in Feb. 2014) is the early favorite to become the 45th U.S. president.*

Those numbers won't survive a partisan election battle, and Democratic challengers may still emerge. The animosity that surrounded her in her first appearance on the national scene, though it has shrunk from sight, has not been eliminated.

But then, she has never been one to dwell too long on the obstacles. In 1969, during her commencement speech at Wellesley, the future Yale Law School stu-

dent spoke on that question. "We arrived at Wellesley and we found, as all of us have found, that there was a gap between expectation and realities," she said. "But it wasn't a discouraging gap and it didn't turn us into cynical, bitter old women at the age of 18. It just inspired us to do something about that gap." More than four decades later, she is still not that bitter old woman. Nor is her story complete.

CAN ANYONE STOP HER?

WHY CLINTON'S 2016 CANDIDACY-WITHOUT-A-CAMPAIGN DOMINATES THE POLITICAL GALAXY BY DAVID VON DREHLE

Hillary Clinton has not decided whether to run for president again. I have this on good authority, despite the barrage of reports detailing the many moves that signal a campaign in the making. People close to Clinton and familiar with her thinking insist that she hasn't made a decision. Moreover, "it's not a decision she is going to make anytime soon," says an insider.

But what about the high-ranking personnel from President Obama's political brain trust who are moving into jobs in pro-Clinton groups? The sources patiently repeat themselves. Clinton, they inform me, has been very busy writing the memoir of her work as secretary of state while also replenishing the coffers of her family's charitable foundation to support her work on behalf of women and children. "She's going to continue to go about her life the way she has chosen to," says the insider. "She's not being coy. When she says she hasn't decided, she hasn't decided."

But what about the email blast that retired general Wesley Clark, a Clinton diehard, sent to past supporters whose names are embedded in Clinton's database, exhorting them to rally to Hillary's cause? "People wanting her to decide, or people getting anxious about it, are working on their own timeline, and frankly there is only one person whose timeline counts," says an increasingly exasperated insider. "Anyway, she could stand on the White House lawn tomorrow and say she wasn't running, and no one would believe her."

Perhaps it all comes down, in Clintonian fashion, to definitions. It depends on the meaning of the word *decide*. And on the meaning of the word *run*. In Hillary Clinton, the United States of America is now experiencing a rare, if not unprecedented, political phenomenon; she requires a new lexicon. Clinton is so globally famous, so politically wired and so primed for the presidency after two campaigns at her husband's side and one epic race of her own that her life as a private citizen has become virtually indistinguishable from her life as a candidate.

We can believe that she hasn't "decided" to "run" because there is almost nothing that a decision would change for her. It would be like Jennifer Aniston deciding to get her picture in a supermarket tabloid or Warren Buffett deciding to be quotable. All outward behaviors remain the same. Whether she raises money from wealthy donors for the Clinton Global Initiative or coaxes cash for a presidential campaign, the canapés and grip-and-grins are identical for Clinton. Her stump speeches while accepting awards for past achievements are barely distinguishable from speeches she might give while collecting endorsements in Iowa

SWING-STATE CRED *Stumping in 2013 for Virginia gubernatorial candidate Terry McAuliffe*

living rooms. The charming handwritten notes she has been showering on far-flung friends serve to nurture political support, whether or not that is the intention, because friendship and politics are inseparable after half a century on the hustings.

Lesser figures—mere governors, senators, vice presidents—face mounting pressure to decide whether to run for president; there are so many pieces to accumulate and put into place. To an astonishing degree, Clinton already has all the pieces: universal name recognition, fervently devoted followers from coast to coast, a robust donor network, legions of experienced counselors, personal mastery of the issues. And she has the cream of two generations of Democratic operatives scrambling to assemble these pieces on her behalf. Her unofficial appara-

tus already includes a grassroots operation, Ready for Hillary, that has raised millions of dollars in predominantly small donations; a "super PAC" called Priorities USA Action, to groom megadonors to fund future air wars; a rapid-response team, Correct the Record, primed to shoot down criticism; a think tank, the Center for American Progress, ready to work up white papers and field-test applause lines; and a women's network, Emily's List, eager to rally the sisterhood to smash the glass ceiling at last.

Clinton has not decided whether to run for president because to do so would only slow her down. Lots of people can be presidential candidates—ask Patrick Buchanan or Dennis Kucinich or Herman Cain. There is only one Hillary able to dominate discussion of 2016 even as she sails above

SUPER-FANS *A ready-made base of women, young people and minorities clamor for Hillary to run.*

it. Indecision serves her well by preserving flexibility in her schedule, by shielding her from answering every Internet controversy and by allowing the Republican opposition to take shape and draw fire.

How long can this go on? Longer than you might think. The typical reasons for a candidate to "decide"—credibility with donors and voters, access to media, ability to recruit staff, leverage to secure endorsements—wouldn't move Clinton, because she already has those things. There's not a door she can't open nor a camera she can't command. Last year, Clinton told interviewer Barbara Walters that she would make a decision in 2014, but some sources in her camp, who generally speak about 2016 only if granted anonymity, suggest that it was a ballpark figure. By saying 2014 while the calendar said 2013, Clinton was merely indi-

cating that her decision was a long way off. "If you polled 25 smart political people and you asked them on a strategic tactical level if a presidential candidate should be doing anything in 2014, they would tell you no," said one insider. "No one in the history of the Republic has started to run this far out."

There's that word again: *run*. We know that Team Clinton actually started running for president sometime in the 1960s, when young Bill fretted about preserving his political viability while avoiding the Vietnam draft. If they ever stopped running, it was only in a semantic sense. Along with her husband, Hillary is the embodiment of the so-called permanent campaign, in which years blur into an endless loop of staged events and solicitations for money and skirmishing for control of the next news cycle. If that's not running, what is?

FIELD MARSHALS *Adam Parkhomenko and Seth Bringman build voter lists and a campaign war chest.*

THE GRAVITY

When Clinton's press secretary, Nick Merrill, answered some questions from TIME about his boss's plans by declaring in an email that "there is no candidate, there is no campaign," I found myself flashing on the image of a black hole—the astrophysical phenomenon that manages to be both invisible and superpowerful at the same time. Scientists confirm the presence of a black hole by measuring its effects on nearby stars as it bends their orbits and heats the gases swirling in its galactic vicinity.

The existence of Clinton's 2016 campaign cannot be directly observed through a formal announcement ritual or by linking to documents at the Federal Election Commission. But its influence on the stars and gases of Washington is unmistakable. Most of her fellow Democrats are signaling

scant interest in taking her on. Massachusetts senator Elizabeth Warren, a hero of the left, has repeatedly said she would not challenge Clinton in the primary. Likewise, senators Kirsten Gillibrand of New York and Amy Klobuchar of Minnesota—who might otherwise vie to be the first female president—have said they would support her candidacy. "I think if another woman ran against Hillary, she would bring down the wrath of women around the country," said a veteran Democratic strategist, echoing a widespread view inside the party that Clinton earned another shot at history when she surrendered gracefully to Barack Obama in 2008.

Vice President Joe Biden would love to run, though he would be 74 by Inauguration Day, and past donors and former staff report that he sees little room for himself in a field with Clinton. Ambitious governors like Martin O'Malley of Maryland, Andrew Cuomo of New York and Deval Patrick of Massachusetts are young enough to wait another cycle or two. To find a Democrat openly courting the race, you have to visit the unlikely terrain of Big Sky Country, where former Montana governor Brian Schweitzer has been enjoying a minor burst of publicity as he flirts with a dark-horse challenge.

This dearth of competition—which could change if Clinton were suddenly, somehow, to appear vulnerable—is a testament to her immense pull inside the Democratic electorate, which is disproportionately female. She has cleared the field of major challengers despite the fact that the party's left wing has serious reservations about her centrist record and gilded connections. In addition to Clinton's fierce detractors on the right, progressive Democrats tend to see her as a hawk on foreign affairs and an enabler of Big Business. Despite this antipathy, however, no fresh figure has emerged to pick up the banner of the left. Only a cantankerous Vermonter, Bernie Sanders, has shown much appetite for the race—and Sanders, a self-described socialist senator, will have to switch parties if he wants to challenge her in the primaries.

In other words, the Stop Hillary movement among Democrats may never get started. As a co-founder of the Progressive Change Campaign Committee, Adam Green might be expected to lead the effort, but Warren's decision to remain on the sidelines has left him resigned to seek concessions from the overwhelming front-runner. Clinton "determines her own fate," Green told Time. "If she embraces things like more Wall Street reform and expanding Social Security benefits instead of cutting them, there will be very little space for a primary challenge of the left."

Toby Chaudhuri, a veteran adviser to progressive Democratic groups, concurs: "There isn't a huge space for a challenger, so the left is really focusing on making sure Clinton is where she needs to be. We'll be paying a lot of attention to where she comes down on issues like privacy, Guantánamo, ending the war in Afghanistan, Syria and others."

She's already making some of the necessary gestures. No longtime Clinton watcher is surprised to find that the noncandidate's noncampaign has been keeping a nonschedule immaculately tuned to the heartstrings of various Democratic constituencies. One day she's delivering a paid speech to clients of the Wall Street bankers at Goldman Sachs; another day finds her at Yale decrying income inequality. When Bill de Blasio was sworn in as New York City's most progressive mayor in decades, Hillary and Bill were conspicuous in the front row—just as they were on hand to celebrate super-moneyman Terry McAuliffe when he took the oath as governor of Virginia. Does she contradict herself? Like Walt Whitman, she contains multitudes.

Of course, she won't be nominated without at least a token challenge. Someone will take the bait, professional Democrats predict, if only to establish credibility as a Clinton running mate or to catch the eyes of publishers, speakers' bureaus and cable networks. "There will be a race because there has to be a race, and it's only good for the party and the candidate to have a race," says Erik Smith, head of Blue Engine Message and Media, a Democratic consulting group. That said, he notes, "The challengers who would worry the Clinton campaign most are all supporting her and have done so early."

Meanwhile, anticipation of a Clinton candidacy is already red hot inside the Beltway, as both parties avert their eyes from a midterm election pitting the dueling faces of an unpopular Congress—the ballot-box

TALK-CIRCUIT STAR *Clinton (at a Feb. 2014 car dealer convention in New Orleans) joked about the last time she drove, in 1996: "I remember it very well. Unfortunately, so does the Secret Service."*

version of shingles vs. flu. Hundreds of operatives from past Clinton campaigns are vying with Obama veterans for positions on what they hope will be the ground floor of something very big. Republicans are launching efforts with names like Stop Hillary 2016 and the Hillary Project, which mix online attacks with spirited fundraising and merchandising appeals in hopes of thwarting Clinton while also cashing in on her galvanizing name. In both parties, Hillary has always been good for business.

THE DECISION

Clinton's luxury of indecision coincides with a phase of presidential politics treasured by insiders. The election is close enough to be real yet far enough away that key factors—the candidates, the state of the economy, the foreign and domestic news—remain blissfully unknowable. Pundits have free rein to make predictions that cannot be checked. One widespread forecast holds that Clinton is poised for a cakewalk of historic proportions.

The theory goes like this: Between his first victory in 2008 and his narrower win in 2012, Obama suffered a significant 4% loss in support from white women. Nevertheless, his strength among minority voters was sufficient to give him a relatively easy re-election victory. Demographic trends indicate that the minority share of the electorate will grow even more by 2016 even as the Republican Party remains split over policies, like immigration reform and voting rights, that might attract those voters. As a result, Clinton is positioned to hold on to Obama's minority support while catalyzing the enthusiasm of women. The combination could produce a landslide.

Veteran Democratic pollster Stanley Greenberg, an old Clinton hand, is among those who argue that the political landscape is highly favorable to Clinton in 2016.

Other party elders are not so sanguine, however. "No matter who we nominate, the Republican theme will be the same: it's time for a change," a senior Democratic strategist told me. "Hillary will be cast as a third term for Obama. They'll try to hang all the trouble with health care on her. And if they manage to put up a serious candidate, we could be in a tough spot." Personal issues will surface, too. Republicans Karl Rove and Sarah Palin have already argued that Clinton's health should be scrutinized, given the severe concussion she suffered when she took a fall in late 2012.

Call it pessimism or call it realism—for nervous Democrats, 2016 looks to be another hard fight across the narrow ground of a few swing states. Broad demographic trends will matter less, they fear, than a relative few hearts and minds in places like Ohio, Pennsylvania and Michigan. Hopeful Republicans are making the same calculation, which is fueling the ambitions of aspirants with strong working-class appeal, men like New Jersey governor Chris Christie, Ohio governor John Kasich and Wisconsin governor Scott Walker. By this analysis, nominee Clinton could find herself—as in 2008—hoisting shots and boasting about her bowling skills in a gritty fight for Rust Belt voters.

This prospect gives her pause, according to sources close to Clinton, and she will be using the coming year to make her own cool-eyed assessment of GOP chances. Like all of her toughest calculations, this will take place inside a tight circle of trusted family and friends: Bill, daughter Chelsea, and longtime staff members Capricia Marshall, Melanne Verveer, Cheryl Mills and Maggie Williams. Not all of them are gung-ho for another campaign. According to a report in Politico, which Clinton sources did not dispute, both Mills and Williams have argued against waging a

READY

NINE CAMPAIGN THEMES HILLARY CLINTON IS TEST-DRIVING

1. YOUTH EMPOWERMENT
'Our country's future depends on healthy kids and loving families. They're the building blocks of a strong and prosperous society.'

JUNE 14, 2013
LAUNCHING THE BILL, HILLARY & CHELSEA CLINTON FOUNDATION'S "TOO SMALL TO FAIL" INITIATIVE IN A VIDEO

2. ECONOMIC INEQUALITY
We must 'reverse this tide of inequality that is eating away at the social fabric of our country.'

OCT. 5, 2013
RECEIVING AN AWARD AT YALE LAW SCHOOL

3. THE WASHINGTON OUTSIDER
'Recently in Washington, unfortunately, we have seen examples of the wrong kind of leadership, when politicians choose scorched earth instead of common ground, when they operate in what I call the "evidence-free zone," with ideology trumping everything else.'

OCT. 19, 2013
ENDORSING VIRGINIA GUBERNATORIAL CANDIDATE AND LONGTIME CLINTON FUNDRAISER TERRY MCAULIFFE

4. SELFLESS AMBITION
'When you think about why people run for office in these times—if it's only about yourself, if it's only about you wanting to get a job and the perks that go with it and having people stand up when you come into the room, that's not enough anymore, because it's hard. Politics is hard.'

OCT. 19, 2013
ENDORSING MCAULIFFE

5. CIVILITY
'We have to be willing to come together as citizens to focus on the kind of future we want, which doesn't include yelling. It includes sitting down and talking with one another.'

OCT. 23, 2013
RESPONDING TO A HECKLER AT THE UNIVERSITY AT BUFFALO

6. FOREIGN INTERVENTION
'We have to be prepared to make the case why we don't have a choice to continue, in some form and fashion, what has worked.'

NOV. 15, 2013
DISCUSSING GAINS MADE FOR AFGHAN WOMEN AND CHILDREN OVER THE PAST DECADE, AT GEORGETOWN UNIVERSITY

7. PROGRESSIVE PRIORITIES
'Ten years ago I was proud to begin working on bipartisan efforts to save unemployment insurance. Let's do it again quickly in this new year.'

DEC. 31, 2013
A TWEET FROM @HILLARYCLINTON

8. HUMAN RIGHTS
'He called me from the van on the way to the hospital and said, "If I were there, I would kiss you." '

OCT. 11, 2013
RECEIVING AN AWARD AT CHATHAM HOUSE, WHERE CLINTON RECOUNTED A PHONE CALL FROM CHINESE ACTIVIST CHEN GUANGCHENG WHEN SHE WAS SECRETARY OF STATE

9. GENDER EQUALITY
'Holding back women is not right, but it is also not smart.'

APRIL 26, 2014
ADDRESSING THE UNITED METHODIST WOMEN ASSEMBLY IN LOUISVILLE, KY.

2016 campaign, while Chelsea has said publicly that she wants her mother to take a break before making any big decisions.

There has never been a would-be presidential candidate with more firsthand knowledge of the grind than Clinton. She knows the toll that campaigns take on candidates and their families; she knows what both victory and defeat feel like; she has had a front-row seat on the burdens and frustrations of the presidency as well as its pomp and power. Putting everything onto the scales, "she would not run just for the sake of running or to be the first woman to win the nomination. She has to believe she can win," a source close to Clinton explained. Some of her supporters might accept second best, "but she is the person who has to run, and she looks at it differently. There has to be a path to victory."

And so, this person added, it remains possible that Clinton could leave the cards of history face-down and walk away from the table. Clinton is not like most politicians, said the source. "She understands better than almost anyone alive that this is a very personal decision about not only her own life but also her family's life." No shred of privacy, if the Clintons have any remaining, would go undisturbed by an ever more inflamed political media, and even in victory her presidency might be stymied by a continuation of partisan gridlock.

At the same time, "she has seen what President Clinton has done in the 13 years since he left office—all the contributions to the public good that have not required him to hold high office. She understands that if you care about making something better, there's more than one job in America where you can do that."

THE STRATEGY

But suppose that she does what Clintons always do and runs anyway? She would enter the race with a suitable bang of delirious rallies and million-dollar checks sometime after the off-year balloting in November. Her advisers say she could be expected to run a campaign that is more tech-savvy behind the scenes than her 2008 effort and more openly targeted toward women. The last time around the track, Clinton soft-pedaled the idea that she was waging a history-making crusade, leaving Obama to seize the symbolic high ground. Her concession speech at the 2008 Democratic Convention, in which she credited her supporters with putting "18 million cracks" in the glass ceiling, made it clear that she would not make the same mistake twice.

Moreover, her record as secretary of state marks her as a particularly macho brand of Democrat. Though former defense secretary Robert Gates caused a stir by revealing in his memoir that Clinton once acknowledged that her opposition to the 2007 troop surge in Iraq was political, a deeper read of Gates's book—along with Clinton's public record and interviews with current and former administration officials—reveals a robust proponent of military intervention.

As head of the State Department, Clinton sided with the generals in favor of a large Afghanistan troop surge. She pressed to arm the Syrian rebels and later endorsed air strikes against the Assad regime. A report from the Senate Intelligence Committee earlier this year faulted her department over security lapses leading up to the 2012 terrorist attack on Americans in Benghazi. But in previous decisions, Clinton's team at State enabled Obama's lethal drone campaign. On at least three crucial issues—the surge in Afghanistan, bombing Libya, and the raid to kill al-Qaeda leader Osama bin Laden—Clinton favored more-aggressive action than Gates himself.

"She is a hawk, but she's a smart hawk," says James Jeffrey, a former ambassador

ENDURING PARTNERS *The Clintons at the 2013 Presidential Medal of Freedom ceremony in Washington*

under President Clinton. Her spokesman, Merrill, prefers the word *pragmatic* but doesn't dispute the larger characterization: "Her approach was always that diplomacy, development and defense were only effective if used together."

Blurring the bright lines of an increasingly polarized public has always been the Clinton family business. Give them the choice of A or B and they'll gravitate to C. Her husband was the Bible-quoting libertine who jogged to McDonald's (before heart disease made him a virtual vegan). He preferred "triangulation" to "false choices"—a trait shared by his wife, the feminist drinking buddy of a spear-rattling John McCain.

Can it play again after all these years? Can a candidate who helped define the 1990s captivate a change-hungry electorate hurtling toward the 2020s? Can the sprawling, inbred, rivalrous soap opera of so many

previous Clinton campaigns be tamed to compete in the sleek and disciplined post-Obama era? Can a divided Democratic Party, with its beleaguered incumbent president, paper over its differences before the divided Republican Party, with its Tea Party dissidents, papers over its own? These are the sorts of questions that hover over a candidate whose path to the White House seems as clear as any in modern memory. There hasn't been a path so bright since Clinton surveyed her future in 2005, before Obama appeared over the horizon.

And there will be answers—eventually—though not at a pace to satisfy the appetite of Washington. Hillary Clinton is master of her own calendar. For the time being, she steers the stars and heats the gases; her unseen candidacy dominates the political galaxy. The timing and nature of the next steps are up to her to decide.

HILLARY BY THE NUMBERS
BREAKING NEW GROUND HAS BEEN A BIG PART OF HER EXTRAORDINARY LIFE

1st student at Wellesley College to give the **commencement address**, in 1969. First woman to become **full partner** at Rose Law Firm. First First Lady to hold a **postgraduate degree** (Yale Law, 1963). First First Lady to run for and be **elected senator** (New York, 2000). First First Lady to **seek the presidency**.

$8,000,000

Advance for her memoir *Living History*

$14,000,000

Reported advance for her new memoir, *Hard Choices*

1964
Became a Goldwater Girl

1968
Became a Democrat

1986
Hillary, then First Lady of Arkansas, became the first woman on the Walmart board of directors

1993
Became the only First Lady to have offices in both the East and West wings of the White House

1996
The Whitewater investigation made her the only First Lady ever to be subpoenaed and compelled to testify before a federal grand jury

$70 **million**
Cost of the seven-year Whitewater investigation

$47 **million**
Spent on investigating Reagan officials involved in the Iran-contra affair

3
Number of presidents she served in an official capacity, tying Eleanor Roosevelt and Lady Bird Johnson

69
Her age on Inauguration Day in 2017, which would make her eight months shy of America's oldest president, Ronald Reagan, who was 69 when he was inaugurated

956,733

Miles she traveled as secretary of state, which equates to this many times traveled around the circumference of the world: **38.42**

112

Number of countries she visited as secretary of state, breaking **Madeleine Albright's record of 99**

$200,000+

Her estimated speaking fee in 2014

---

5 foot 6

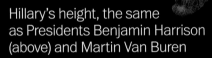

Hillary's height, the same as Presidents Benjamin Harrison (above) and Martin Van Buren

---

Only

First Lady to **win a Grammy Award**, for the spoken-word version of her book *It Takes a Village*. Only woman to earn **front-runner status** for a major party's presidential nomination. Only woman to be a **presidential candidate** in every primary in every state

---

'ALTHOUGH WE WEREN'T ABLE TO SHATTER THAT HIGHEST, HARDEST GLASS CEILING THIS TIME, THANKS TO YOU, IT'S GOT ABOUT 18 MILLION CRACKS IN IT, AND THE LIGHT IS SHINING THROUGH LIKE NEVER BEFORE, FILLING US ALL WITH THE HOPE AND THE SURE KNOWLEDGE THAT THE PATH WILL BE A LITTLE EASIER NEXT TIME.'

Hillary's concession speech on June 7, 2008. Before she dropped out of the race for the Democratic presidential nomination, she got 17,857,501 votes, the most of any woman to run for any U.S. office

EVOLUTION OF A LEADER

HOW A TEEN REPUBLICAN BECAME A FEMINIST ICON
AND AN ACTIVIST WITH BIG AMBITIONS BY ALEX ALTMAN

COLLEGE LIFE
Clinton (at Wellesley in 1969) underwent a dramatic political transformation.

H

Hillary Clinton has lived so many public lives that it can be easier to embrace the caricatures than the complexity. Over the past 45 years, Clinton has been a teen Republican, a feminist icon as a college student, an activist First Lady and a conservative bugbear. She was a hardworking senator, a ubiquitous secretary of state and a onetime (and perhaps future) presidential frontrunner. But if you want to cut through the cartoons and mythmaking to understand the woman behind it all, it helps to go back to the Middle American beginnings of her extraordinary story.

Hillary Diane Rodham was born in Chicago on Oct. 26, 1947. She was the oldest of three children raised by the former Dorothy Howell, a homemaker, and Hugh Rodham, the owner of a small but prosperous drapery-fabric business.

At age 3, Hillary moved with her parents and infant brother to Park Ridge, a relatively affluent suburb about 15 miles northwest of the Loop. She grew up in a two-story brick house with a screened-in porch and a pair of sundecks, which her father purchased for $35,000 in cash. Park Ridge was the picture of postwar Americana, with leafy streets and spacious sidewalks abutting comfortable homes with tidy lawns. As Hillary recounts it, hers was a typical and happy middle-class childhood. She was a tomboy—fond of bike rides, the Chicago Cubs, ice skating and softball games with neighborhood kids.

Hillary's parents emphasized academic achievement and drilled her in reading and math. At school she was a teacher's pet. In a break with the era's gender norms, her mother and father encouraged her to play games with the boys and insisted she set lofty professional goals. (One of her early aspirations was to become an astronaut.) She held part-time jobs from an early age and was raised to be self-sufficient. The lessons took. "I grew up in a cautious, conformist era in American history," Hillary wrote in her memoir *Living History*. "But in the midst of our *Father Knows Best* upbringing, I was taught to resist peer pressure."

Yet Clinton's childhood was hardly blissful. Hugh Rodham was a domineering presence at home. He was sometimes mean and always miserly; one household rule held that the heat was turned off overnight to save on bills, which often meant the children were left shivering in their beds. If Hillary left a tube of toothpaste unscrewed, he would hurl the cap out the bathroom

THE PRIDE OF PARK RIDGE
Hillary Rodham (clockwise from top left) as a toddler, around age 6, as a high school senior and around age 11

window and force her to retrieve it from the yard. "My father was always strict with his kids," she wrote, "but he was much harder on the boys than on me."

One of the ironies of Hillary Clinton's reputation on the right is that she grew up a Republican. Though her mother was ostensibly a Democrat, her own beliefs were shaped by the conservative politics of her father, a staunch anticommunist who believed in personal discipline and fiscal responsibility. In high school she was a Goldwater Girl who volunteered during the 1964 presidential campaign to canvass black neighborhoods on the South Side of Chicago, attempting to suss out signs of voter fraud. "I liked Senator Goldwater," she wrote later, "because he was a rugged individualist who swam against the tide. Years later, I admired his outspoken support of individual rights, which he considered consistent with his old-fashioned conservative principles." She served a stint on the student council during high school, an early sign of the political acumen that would come to define her.

She was also a woman of faith from a young age. Hillary actively participated at a local Methodist church and attended Bible classes. During high school, she formed a mentoring relationship with a young reverend, Don Jones, who would remain a frequent correspondent into her college career. The minister, she wrote in *Living History*, aided her "quest to reconcile my father's insistence on self-reliance and my mother's concerns about social justice." In 1961 Jones took Hillary to visit inner-city youth groups in Chicago for a glimpse of life outside prosperous Park Ridge. A year later, he brought her to hear a sermon by Martin Luther King Jr., which opened her eyes to the political turmoil roiling the nation outside her high-school bubble. "Until then, I had been dimly aware of the

social revolution occurring in our country," she wrote in her autobiography, "but Dr. King's words illuminated the struggle taking place and challenged our indifference."

HER POLITICAL EVOLUTION

As an academic standout, Hillary had her pick of elite universities. In the fall of 1965, she arrived at Wellesley College in Massachusetts, one of the nation's top all-women schools. Hillary showed up on campus toting a tattered copy of Goldwater's *The Conscience of a Conservative*; as a freshman, she became president of the school's Young Republicans club. But the social upheaval sweeping the nation, from the ascendancy of the feminist and civil rights movements to the antiwar protests spawned by Vietnam, would ultimately blow away her old beliefs. "Since Xmas vacation, I've gone through three and a half metamorphoses," she wrote to a male pen pal in the spring of her sophomore year, "and am beginning to feel as though there is a smorgasbord of personalities spread before me."

She was grappling with a slow but steady political evolution, growing alienated from the conservative positions on social issues and foreign policy. At first she gravitated toward the GOP's moder-

'BY THE TIME I WAS A COLLEGE JUNIOR, I HAD GONE FROM BEING A GOLDWATER GIRL TO SUPPORTING THE ANTI-WAR CAMPAIGN OF EUGENE MCCARTHY.'

GENERATIONAL LEADER *The 1969 Wellesley class president was featured in* Life *magazine.*

ate wing, headed by New York governor Nelson Rockefeller. Until late in her college career, she remained nominally a Republican, spending a summer on Capitol Hill as an intern for the House Republican conference. In 1968 alone, she attended the Republican convention in Miami, at which Richard Nixon was nominated to her dismay, and drove to New Hampshire to volunteer for the presidential bid of the antiwar Democratic senator Eugene McCarthy. In a letter to a friend during her college years, she described herself as a "mind conservative and a heart liberal."

King's assassination was a watershed event, and Hillary returned to campus from a demonstration after the civil rights leader's death wearing a black armband, increasingly certain she wanted to devote her life to effecting social change. "By the

time I was a college junior," she wrote, "I had gone from being a Goldwater Girl to supporting the anti-war campaign of Eugene McCarthy." During her senior year, she wrote a 92-page honors thesis on the left-wing community organizer Saul Alinsky, whose political manifesto, *Rules for Radicals*, has made him a contemporary bête noire for the conservative movement.

It was at Wellesley that she became a star. She was elected president of the student body after a characteristically diligent door-knocking campaign. In that role she displayed a penchant for building consensus. She worked with school administrators to organize safe public demonstrations against the Vietnam War while ensuring that the protests wouldn't devolve into riots, as was happening on campuses across the country. "She kept the student body focused

on learning about the war, the pros and cons, being able to discuss it," her faculty adviser, professor Alan Schechter, has said.

At her graduation in 1969 she was made the school's first student commencement speaker, an honor over which "there was no debate," said Wellesley president Ruth Adams. Hillary's speech was partly a critical response to the address delivered by Wellesley's other commencement speaker, the sitting Massachusetts senator Edward Brooke—a moderate black Republican whose election she had supported. Her remarks were introspective and searching, probing for a synthesis between the liberal ethos animating the campus and her own conservative upbringing. "There's a very strange conservative strain that goes through a lot of New Left, collegiate protests," she told the crowd. "It harkens back to a lot of the old virtues, to the fulfillment of original ideas." The speech was polarizing; some bristled at the spectacle of a female student rebuking a political star. But it garnered national attention. Soon after, *Life* magazine included a photo spread of then 21-year-old Hillary—clad in leather sandals and baggy pinstriped pants—as an emblem of college life.

Peers began to whisper that this confident woman wearing John Lennon spectacles could one day be president. "The accolades and attacks turned out to be a preview of things to come," she writes in *Living History*. "I have never been as good or as bad as my most fervid supporters and opponents claimed."

THE DEFINING EVENT

Thus anointed as a future leader, Hillary enrolled at Yale Law School in the fall of

WEDDING DAY *After several rejected proposals from Bill, Hillary married her "force of nature" on Oct. 11, 1975.*

1969. Swept in by the tide of the women's rights movement, she was among the first large wave of women to matriculate at Yale. The owner of a freshly minted degree in political science, she had decided to pursue a legal career, she recalls, because she saw the law as an instrument of social justice. During her time in New Haven, she took up a series of causes, including children's advocacy, that would become abiding interests throughout her career. She arrived in law school at the apex of the '60s counterculture. The main quad at New Haven was declared a "liberated zone" her first year by the campus's motley collection of antiwar advocates and left-wing activists.

Hillary fell in with a group of progressive students and spent her first year at Yale advocating for causes such as lowering the voting age from 21 to 18. She introduced herself to a future mentor, Marian Wright Edelman, who would later give her a job at the Children's Defense Fund in Boston. On a campus where the brightest students jockey for selection to the law review, Hillary opted instead to join an alternative journal dedicated to social action. She plunged into a variety of social-justice internships, working to combat cases of child abuse in New Haven and spending a summer dedicated to helping migrant workers at Democratic senator Walter Mondale's Washington office.

The defining event of her life came in the fall of her second year at Yale. The first time she spied Bill Clinton, he was telling a group of students about how Arkansas grew the biggest watermelons in the world. He was a striking presence even then, fresh from a stint at Oxford and sporting an unruly reddish beard that made him look "more like a Viking than a Rhodes Scholar," she wrote. They crossed paths early that semester, in the

Yale law library. But they didn't spend time together until the following spring, when Bill bumped into Hillary as she made her way to the registrar's office to sign up for next fall's classes. He accompanied her on the false pretense of having to do the same.

"I laughed when he confessed that he just wanted to spend time with me," she recalled in her autobiography, "and we went for a long walk that turned into our first date." He wheedled their way into a Rothko exhibit at the school art gallery, which happened to be closed. They didn't become a couple right away; she had a boyfriend at the time. But when she decamped for a summer job at a law firm in Oakland, he decided to come along, spurning an offer to work in the South as an organizer for George McGovern's presidential campaign.

They moved in together in Berkeley, and again when they returned to New Haven the next fall. That summer she joined him at McGovern's Texas headquarters in Austin, their first stint together in the crucible of a national campaign. When they graduated, Clinton took her to England to tour some of his former haunts. It was on that trip, on the shores of a British lake at twilight, that he first asked her to marry him.

She said no. He was a budding politician, determined to return to his native Arkansas to run for office. She was a smart young attorney with a glittering résumé that could open any door in Washington or New York. And theirs was a tumultuous relationship, intense and volcanic. Clinton was a womanizer even then, and Hillary was unsure she wanted to subjugate her career ambitions to his and accompany a husband to a political backwater like Arkansas. He asked her to marry him several times. On each occasion, she declined.

He returned home to Arkansas, teaching at the law school in Fayetteville to mark time before a run for Congress. In 1974 she headed to Washington for a plum gig as a staff attorney on the House Judiciary Committee investigating the Watergate scandal. (The job was first offered to Bill, who recommended his future wife instead.) Hillary worked seven days a week, holed up with fellow lawyers inside a hotel on Capitol Hill, researching the case for Nixon's impeachment. All the while, she maintained a relationship with her "force of nature" boyfriend in Arkansas, insisting to friends that he would become president one day. When Nixon resigned the presidency in Aug. 1974, Hillary could have eased into a prestigious job elsewhere in the capital. Instead, to the disbelief of friends, she headed south. She wanted to be with Bill. "I chose to follow my heart," she wrote, "instead of my head."

Hillary Rodham arrived in Fayetteville, Ark., in the late summer of 1974. Bill Clinton was turning toward the homestretch of his first congressional campaign. Just six months after graduating from law school, he had mounted a campaign to unseat a popular Republican incumbent, John Paul

THEY DROVE TO A SMALL BRICK HOUSE THAT SHE HAD MENTIONED SHE LIKED. 'I BOUGHT IT,' HE SAID, 'SO NOW YOU'D BETTER MARRY ME.'

TEAM WORK *The Clintons vote to win back the Arkansas governor's seat in Nov. 1982.*

Hammerschmidt, in the Natural State's Third District. Hillary assumed a senior strategist role at his campaign headquarters as he crisscrossed rural swathes of the district to court voters. A race forecast as a cakewalk turned into a nail-biter. In the end, Clinton lost his first campaign by about 6,000 votes, garnering 48% of the vote. But the narrow defeat against a formidable incumbent marked him as a rising star.

Hillary picked up a teaching job at the law school, where she was regarded as a tough and talented professor. To her surprise, she found she liked the rhythms of Fayetteville; she rooted for the Razorbacks football team and formed a variety of close friendships. Her relationship with Clinton remained turbulent, and she wavered on whether she wanted to marry him.

A MARRIAGE OF EQUALS
Finally, in the summer of 1975, he picked her up at the airport when she returned from a trip to explore potential job prospects on the East Coast. They drove to a small brick house in Fayetteville that she had mentioned she liked. "I bought it," he told her, "so now you'd better marry me." This time she agreed. They were married on Oct. 11, 1975, in a ceremony held in the living room of their new house. Hillary, who decided to keep her last name, wore a lace Victorian dress purchased only the

HAPPY WARRIORS
Hillary and Bill (with Chelsea) on the stump at a 1982 Labor Day parade.

night before. "After all that has happened since, I'm often asked why Bill and I have stayed together," she writes in *Living History*. "What can I say to explain a love that has persisted for decades and has grown through our shared experiences of parenting a daughter, burying our parents and tending our extended families, a lifetime's worth of friends, a common faith and an abiding commitment to our country?"

The following year, Clinton won his first election, becoming Arkansas attorney general at the age of 30. Forgoing early notions of a career in public-interest law, Hillary decided to accept a job at a prestigious corporate firm in Little Rock, the Rose Law Firm. While some of its lawyers bristled at her hiring, she would become the firm's first female partner.

She was the family's primary breadwinner as Bill climbed the political ladder. In a Southern culture that still looked askance at a woman who pursued a high-powered career, Hillary was driven and ambitious. In addition to her law career, she served on corporate boards, including that of Walmart. And she played key strategic roles in shaping her husband's campaigns, including his first successful run for the governor's office in 1978.

Concerned about subsisting on her husband's meager public servant's salary, she even dabbled in volatile commodities markets. Tutored by a friend, she began swapping cattle futures. Though she once lost $16,000 in a single trade—about half her husband's annual wages at the time— she proved a skilled investor. Scared off by the swings, she shuttered her account within about a year, but by then Hillary had notched a $99,000 profit. Around the

A NEW SURNAME *In Feb. 1982 Hillary Rodham became Mrs. Bill Clinton and reclaimed her First Lady title.*

same time, her taste for speculative investments led the Clintons, along with two friends, to purchase 230 acres of undeveloped land along the White River in the Arkansas Ozarks. This failed $200,000 Whitewater deal would later become the centerpiece of an exhaustive congressional investigation, as well as a byword on the right for alleged Clintonian cronyism. (Neither Hillary nor Bill Clinton was ever charged; investigators concluded that there was insufficient evidence of wrongdoing on the part of either.)

Not everyone in Arkansas was enamored of Arkansas's new First Lady. As her profile grew, Hillary became an increasingly a polarizing figure—a role that foreshadowed the venom that would envelop her in Washington years later. In his first year as governor, Bill appointed her to head his health-care advisory committee, another harbinger of the battles to come. Some observers found her outsize role in shaping policy distasteful. Others whispered about her decision not to take his name. She was not a typical First Lady, more governing partner than supportive spouse.

Consternation over Hillary's public role deepened even amid the birth of Chelsea in 1980. Later that year, Bill Clinton ran for re-election in a dismal climate for Democrats, marked by class resentments and voter disfavor at the flailing presidency of Jimmy Carter. He had accomplished little thus far in the two-year term granted by the state's constitution and had made more than a few foes. His decision to pay for highway improvement by hiking cartag fees sparked a public outcry. Clinton's Republican opponent, Frank White, tried to court conservatives irked by the feminist First Lady by hammering Hillary's decision to keep her last name. In Nov. 1980, the Clintons were ousted from the governor's mansion. Hillary was convinced she had hampered the campaign. "I was an oddity because of my dress, my Northern ways and the use of my maiden name," she wrote.

When he ran again two years later, Hillary was determined to play the role of the dutiful political spouse. She began calling herself Hillary Rodham Clinton for the first time. "I decided it was more important for Bill to be Governor than for me to keep my maiden name," she explained in *Living History*. When he ran to retake the governorship in 1982, Hillary stumped doggedly on his behalf and served as the strategic mastermind behind his political resurrection. "She was out in front, on the campaign trail, and in charge. She had an opinion on everything," said campaign aide Woody Bassett, according to Hillary's biographer Carl Bernstein. "Issues. People. Where Bill was going to speak. I mean everything." Hillary knew that her husband's next race would be pivotal. He was telegenic, Southern and skilled at forging connections with voters—attributes that marked him as a rising force within the Democratic Party. But she knew that a third lost election would dim his political star and relegate him to the party's second string.

Chastened by defeat and determined to avoid repeating their mistakes, the Clintons recaptured the governorship in a rout, winning 55% of the vote. He was the first chief executive in the state's history to be ousted from office and then return to win it a second time. Bill and Hillary Clinton held onto the mansion in Little Rock for another decade, their national profile growing all the while. And then, in 1992, it was time to trade up to a bigger house and a bigger job.

INAUGURAL BALL *The Clintons (with Chelsea, age 6, in 1987) kick off their fourth term as Arkansas's First Family.*

WHITE HOUSE LESSONS

FIVE KEY THINGS THAT HILLARY LEARNED, SOMETIMES THE HARD WAY, DURING EIGHT YEARS AS FIRST LADY BY MICHAEL CROWLEY

TEAM CLINTON
The Clintons and Gores kick off the 1993 inaugural with a rollicking concert on the Mall.

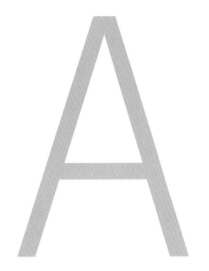

America has had powerful First Ladies throughout its history, but it had never seen a First Lady as influential as Hillary Clinton was during her eight years in the White House. Certainly there has never been a more controversial one. From virtually the moment she arrived in Washington, until and beyond the day she departed, she was the target of almost nonstop scrutiny and criticism from conservatives, prosecutors, reporters and tabloid gossips— along with the sustaining love of a passionate base of admirers.

After a campaign in which her husband had promised voters they would be getting "two for the price of one"—in effect a co-presidency—Hillary took a high-profile role right away, leading Bill Clinton's signature health-care reform effort. At the same time, she was also the focus of multiple legal, political and media queries into subjects ranging from her legal work in Arkansas to her personal finances to staff shake-ups in the White House, as well

as more lurid rumormongering about her personal life.

Hillary's visible policy role receded quickly after health care went down in flames, and she spent the rest of her White House tenure focused on less-controversial women's and children's issues.

But the controversy and scrutiny roared back with the arrival of Monica Lewinsky as a household name in 1998. In tandem with a political debate about Bill Clinton's impeachment came a raging social debate about the choices the wives of cheating husbands make, and Hillary's ultimate decision to stay married to Bill. Though that choice had its share of fierce critics, Clinton's approval ratings hit all-time highs of nearly 70% in the aftermath of the Lewinsky scandal. That set the stage for a successful run in 1999 and 2000 for the Senate from the state of New York. But even then she would leave Washington on a dimmer note, tainted by outrage over last-minute pardons granted by her husband, including four to people with financial ties to her brothers, Hugh and Tony. (Hugh later returned a $400,000 legal fee from two of the pardoned felons.)

If it had been a grueling eight years in the White House, those years also equipped her with some valuable lessons about politics, Washington and public life.

1. CHANGE IS REALLY, REALLY HARD

Before there was Obamacare, there was Hillarycare. Soon after Bill Clinton took office in 1993, he put his wife in charge of a task force charged with overhauling the U.S. health-care system. When Hillary Clinton set up shop in a West Wing office,

POWER COUPLE *In 1993 the new First Lady and the 42nd president began an eight-year tenure in the White House that would bring them breathtaking highs and lows.*

LEADING THE CHARGE *Hillary (at a Sept. 1993 rally) was deputized to reform U.S. health care.*

it was a clear sign that she would have more policy influence than any First Lady before her.

Hillary never thought that remaking the health-care system, and providing coverage to the millions of Americans who lacked it, would be easy. But she didn't expect the effort to result in a scathing political loss, one that taught her a hard lesson. "I still have the scars to show for it," she told an audience in 2007. "I needed some health care after that was over."

Clinton approached the huge task in a style that has since become familiar: immersing herself in the policy and mastering the details of its substance. Early on, there were some good signs— she won positive reviews for her Capitol Hill testimony on behalf of the plan, as well as for her backroom schmooz-

ing of congressional power brokers.

But the storyline quickly turned sour. Her management of the bill-writing process was criticized as secretive and arrogant; opponents successfully cast the 1,368-page bill that her task force submitted as an attempt to force a complicated scheme on the country without adequate debate. When hundreds of protesters turned out at a July 1994 rally to promote the plan in Seattle, the Secret Service convinced Hillary to wear a bulletproof vest. The effort finally petered out in the fall, setting the stage for a disastrous midterm election in which Republicans won both chambers of Congress for the first time in four decades.

While health care's defeat had plenty of factors behind it—including ferocious opposition from conservatives and powerful health-care interests—Hillary's

FIGHTING THE CHARGE *Seven months later, she fielded tough questions about Whitewater.*

prominent role was one of them. At the time, she decried the "personal, vicious hatred" aimed at her husband and herself. But Clinton has since accepted some of the blame. "On bad days, I faulted myself for botching health care," she later wrote, "coming on too strong and galvanizing our opponents."

But the issue was about more than personality, wrote Clinton in her 2003 memoir *Living History*: "Our most critical mistake," she said, "was trying to do too much, too fast."

In sum, Clinton, who had little Washington experience before arriving at the White House, came away from the health-care debacle with a new appreciation for how hard change is to enact there. Whatever momentum and implied mandate her husband's election had entailed, it

meant little against powerful organized opposition on Capitol Hill and expensive industry-funded TV ad campaigns.

Clinton seemed to refer back to these experiences during her 2008 presidential campaign, particularly when she implied that Barack Obama's promises of sweeping change reflected a naiveté about how Washington really works. "Now, I could stand up here and say, 'Let's get everybody together, let's get unified, the sky will open, the light will come down, celestial choirs will be singing ... and the world will be perfect,'" Clinton said at a Feb. 2008 campaign event. "But I have no illusions about how hard [governing] is going to be. You are not going to wave a magic wand and make the special interests disappear."

It was a lesson the Clintons were not the last to learn.

PRESIDENTIAL POOCH *Bill Clinton once joked that he needed "one loyal friend in Washington." Enter Buddy (in 1998).*

2. AMERICA SHOULD LEAD THE WORLD, WITH FORCE WHEN NECESSARY

Like her husband, Hillary Clinton arrived in Washington with no formal foreign-policy experience. In her career as an Arkansas lawyer she had shown no strong interest in the world beyond America's borders. Her husband was elected on a domestic platform heavily focused on health care and the economy. But over her eight years in the White House, Hillary developed a belief in the uses of American power—one that would eventually incur major damage to her political ambitions.

As early as 1993, Hillary has recounted, she believed that the U.S. should intervene in the Balkans to protect innocent victims of the disintegration of the former Yugoslavia. "I was convinced that the only way to stop the genocide in Bosnia was through selective air strikes against Serbian targets," Hillary wrote in *Living History*. It was another two years before her husband would order military action.

Clinton has also said that she persuaded her husband to initiate a U.S.-led NATO bombing campaign in Kosovo in 1999 to protect Kosovar Muslims from slaughter at the hands of Serbian nationalists. "I urged him to bomb," she told *Talk* magazine. "You cannot let this go on at the end of a century that has seen the major holocaust of our time. What do we have NATO for if not to defend our way of life?"

That line was an echo of her foreign-affairs mentor Madeleine Albright, who served as secretary of state in Bill Clinton's second term. "What's the point of having this superb military you're always talking about if we can't use it?" Albright had once asked Colin Powell, then the chairman of the Joint Chiefs of Staff, who was highly cautious about U.S. military action. The descendant of Holocaust survivors, Al-

bright felt America had a special responsibility to protect foreign victims of aggression. That was a worldview she ingrained in her close friend Hillary Clinton, with whom Albright had what she later called an "unprecedented partnership," which included regular meetings to talk policy at the State Department. "I was once asked whether it was appropriate for the two of us to work together so closely," Albright wrote in her 2005 memoir. "I agreed that it was a departure from tradition."

Hillary praised the use of foreign policy to promote democracy abroad. "I am very pleased that this president and administration have made democracy one of the centerpieces of our foreign policy," she said in 1999.

That notion grew more controversial after it became a central theme for George W. Bush. But in conjunction with her belief that U.S. military force could be used for positive ends, it may have influenced her fateful Oct. 2002 Senate vote to authorize the use of force against Iraq.

More than anything, that vote may have cost Hillary a chance at the 2008 Democratic nomination. But even as Obama's secretary of state, she continued to advocate for foreign interventions, from Libya to Syria to Afghanistan—carrying the foreign-policy worldview she developed during the 1990s into the 21st century.

3. DON'T TRUST THE MEDIA

Like most politicians, Hillary has long had a complex relationship with the press. Reporters were understandably thrilled to watch the first baby-boomer woman try to fit into the old-fashioned, almost Edwardian post of First Lady. And Mrs. Clinton frequently employed that curiosity to good effect. But, like other public figures before her, she soon found it difficult to manage the press on her own terms.

MORALE BOOSTER *The First Lady visits U.S. peacekeepers in tense Northern Bosnia in 1995.*

By many accounts, Clinton has long felt that the media was, if not the enemy, certainly not her friend. People close to Hillary say she believes that it too eagerly pounces on rumor and misinformation and places a good "scandal" ahead of the facts. She arrived in the White House in 1993 already seething over coverage of her husband's alleged past extramarital affairs and financial dealings. According to then–White House press secretary George Stephanopoulos, Hillary pushed a plan during her first days in the White House to limit the press corps' access to the West Wing.

And as reporters pursued stories about the Clintons' investments in an Arkansas real estate venture known as Whitewater, Hillary supported a stonewall strategy. She insisted on rejecting a 1993 request from the *Washington Post* for personal financial documents from the couple—even though her husband agreed with advisers who felt it was best to avoid the appearance of a cover-up. David Gergen, a former adviser to the Clinton White House, later called Hillary's refusal to turn over the documents "the decisive turning point" in the Whitewater saga, fueling a belief that the Clintons were hiding something.

The distrust between the First Lady and the guardians of the First Amendment deepened when Clinton established herself and her staff in what came to be known as "Hillaryland," a suite of offices in what was then called the Old Executive Office Building (EOB) next to the White House. (Most First Ladies had, until the Clintons arrived, worked out of the quieter, less central East Wing of the White House.) During much of the first term, many presidential policies

Clinton marks Black History Month at a Washington, D.C., school, 1997.

and speeches seemed to make a pit stop in the First Lady's warren of interconnected rooms in the Old EOB. Reporters believed that fact made her staff and her input worthy of close coverage; Clinton did not always see it that way. Her attitude in the first term may have been summed up in notes recorded by one of her best friends from Arkansas, Diane Blair, and recently made public. "Just visited with Hillary," Blair wrote in 1995. "I told her how fascinating I found the latest spate of Hillary-at-two-years stories, and she expressed her total exasperation with all this obsession and attention, and how hard she's finding it to conceal her contempt for it all." Blair wrote that Clinton thought the press "has big egos and no brains."

Her husband's second term hardly improved Hillary's feelings toward the press.

Although she came to accept her husband's guilt in the Monica Lewinsky affair, she felt that the mainstream media had been manipulated by conservatives using personal scandal in an ideological effort to destroy her husband's presidency.

Hillary's White House years left an enduring hostility toward the press within her political machine. To this day, Hillary Clinton benefits from more than her share of positive press. But when it comes to the media, she never for a moment lets her guard down.

4. THERE IS A VAST RIGHT-WING CONSPIRACY

The first news that Bill Clinton had an affair with Monica Lewinsky broke on the website the Drudge Report in Jan. 1998. Several days later, Hillary sat for an

WHITEWATER AGONISTES
The First Lady at a press conference before testifying in front of a federal grand jury in early 1996

Monica Lewinsky (center, in Oct. 1996) also saw Bill in the Oval Office.

interview on the *Today* show, where she issued a now-famous declaration. "The great story here for anybody willing to find it and write about it and explain it," Clinton told NBC's Matt Lauer, "is this vast right-wing conspiracy that has been conspiring against my husband since the day he announced for president."

The notion of a "vast right-wing conspiracy" was as controversial as it was quotable. Both supporters and critics said that Clinton—who at that time still believed her husband's denials of any affair—was diverting attention from her husband's behavior to sinister but nebulous enemies. It looked embarrassing in hindsight, after it emerged that her husband really had committed adultery in the Oval Office. But it served a political benefit, by making her husband's infidelity into a political cause for liberals.

It also reflected Clinton's conviction that she and her husband had been the targets of an unusually personal campaign of attacks from conservatives. The Clintons watched publications funded by wealthy conservatives, including the *American Spectator* and the *Washington Times*, report questionably sourced stories that then leapt into the mainstream media.

Five years later, Clinton wrote that she "might have phrased my point more artfully." But, she added, "I do believe there was, and still is, an interlocking network of groups and individuals" using money and influence to fight the liberal agenda, including through the "politics of personal destruction."

To some degree, this has become standard fare on both sides of the political spectrum. The rise of cable television

IN THE END *The First Lady stood by her husband, though the affair nearly cost him the presidency.*

and the Internet has created an explosion of partisan media, on both left and right, often funded by wealthy benefactors with strong ideological agendas.

Still, Clinton's allies believe that no other politician draws the sort of organized and coordinated attacks that she does. They see an all-too-familiar dynamic playing out in the conservative media's fixation with the Sept. 2012 attack on a U.S. diplomatic compound in Benghazi, Libya, that claimed four American lives. "In a nutshell, Benghazi's not a scandal, it's a hoax," wrote the pro-Clinton journalist David Brock.

One difference from the 1990s is that the Clinton machine has what you might call its own counterconspiracy. Since her departure from the State Department, Clinton has been defended by an array of aggressive websites and well-funded political groups that respond quickly and sharply to her critics. In an ironic twist, the website Media Matters for America is run by Brock, a former conservative journalist turned Clinton ally who wrote critical articles about the Clintons for right-leaning publications. Since his political conversion, Brock has said that Clinton's use of the word "vast" might have been an exaggeration but that he personally witnessed the "conspiracy" to damage her and her husband in the 1990s.

5. 'SOLDIER ON'

Anyone who spends decades in the public eye learns to ride out the ups and downs. But few have seen so many, and to such extremes, as the Clintons. From her own experience and her husband's, she has learned that politics is a long game that requires perseverance—and a very tough hide.

"One of the best pieces of advice I've ever heard is from Eleanor Roosevelt . . . who said that women in politics or public roles should grow skin like a rhinoceros," Clinton told an audience in Feb. 2014.

Clinton has described the anguish she felt when things were going badly in the White House. During a meeting with her staff after the disastrous 1994 midterm elections, she fought back tears as she apologized for her mistakes and said she was considering withdrawing from an active political role. Her staff talked her out of it, and Hillary says she adopted the phrase "soldier on" as a kind of motto.

And so she did. Her public approval rating crashed along with health care, to below 50% in the mid-1990s. But then it soared to new heights as Americans sympathized with her during the Lewinsky scandal—before diving once again at the end of her husband's presidency.

The public-opinion roller coaster would continue for years to come, but her White House years had conditioned her to such twists of fate. Some people had trouble understanding how Hillary could refuse to quit the 2008 Democratic presidential race after she fell far behind Barack Obama. But they didn't understand the "soldier on" mentality she'd developed as First Lady.

"It's important to learn how to take criticism seriously but not personally," Clinton told her friend Diane Blair. "That is not an easy task. I can tell you that from many years of experience and a lot of missteps along the way."

GENDER EQUALITY *Hillary and civil rights pioneer Dorothy Height listen to the president speak at a 1998 event advocating equal pay for women.*

THE SENATE OVERACHIEVER

HER CELEBRITY HELPED GET HER THE JOB,
BUT IT WAS HER HARD WORK THAT WON OVER
HER COLLEAGUES BY ZEKE MILLER

PHOTO ILLUSTRATION BY ALBERT WATSON

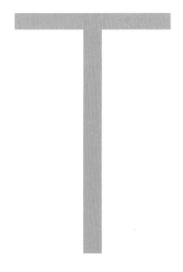Ten yards from the reserved Senators Only elevator, Hillary Clinton hit her first roadblock: a woman visiting from upstate New York, a Wall Street stockbroker, then a delegation from Kyrgyzstan. The senator had been in office for just a few weeks in early 2001, and already aides were caught off guard by the waves of people stopping their boss in the gilded hallways of the Capitol. The walking time between hearings, typically reserved by other senators for quick briefings from staff, was for her an exercise in handshaking and photo-ops. The new senator, though, shrugged it off. She smiled at the tourist, took the stockbroker's business card and handed the Kyrgyzstanis' gift of a wooden doll to an aide, making her way into the elevator and her next subcommittee hearing. "We're learning all the rules of the Senate," she said, "and then those that apply to me."

Therein lay the golden rule of Senator Hillary: first, do no harm; and its corollary: don't ever appear entitled.

The first First Lady to pursue a political career of her own, Clinton's decision to fill legendary New York senator Daniel Patrick Moynihan's seat reeked at first of privilege and opportunism. She announced her intention to run even before she had a place to live in the state, buying a $1.7 million home in the tony New York suburban hamlet of Chappaqua two months after launching an exploratory bid for the seat. Perhaps more troubling in the sports mecca, she donned a Yankees hat and spoke of a lifelong allegiance to the Bronx Bombers despite her well-known affinity for the Chicago Cubs.

On the same day the Senate was voting on her husband's impeachment, Clinton was meeting with longtime adviser Harold Ickes to lay the groundwork for a potential campaign. She wrote later, "The most difficult decisions I have made in my life were to stay married to Bill and to run for the Senate from New York." The president was supportive, relishing the chance to get back to campaigning. "For 20 years we've gone where I wanted to go and done what I wanted to do, and I'll give you the next 20 years," he recounted in a speech to his wife's donors. "And if I'm still alive after that, we'll fight over the rest."

Guided by longtime consultants Mandy Grunwald and Mark Penn, Clinton hired as campaign manager the future New York City mayor Bill de Blasio, at the time a relatively unknown community activist, who plotted out a strategy designed to bring her down to earth. The big presidential-style rallies she held for her husband were replaced by small-scale listening sessions in diners and living rooms across the state. To overcome the carpetbagger charge, she

PROUD MOMENT *Bill, Chelsea, and Al Gore, in a reenactment for posterity of Hillary's Senate oath*

visited all 62 counties in a Ford conversion van the press nicknamed the HRC Speed-wagon, comparing rural upstate New York with back home in Arkansas, outworking her Republican opponent, the unheralded congressman Rick Lazio from Long Island. Lazio was thrust into the race after New York mayor Rudy Giuliani dropped out amid a personal and political maelstrom (and a diagnosis of prostate cancer). Hillary pledged to forge "bipartisan coalitions" beginning on her first day in the Senate, as Lazio, in making his campaign about the Clinton White House scandals, managed to appear to be the tired candidate. He rarely ventured outside his downstate enclave. Clinton's uncharacteristically small-scale campaign, combined with 100% name recognition, was integral to her victory.

Out of that race emerged the paradox that would define Clinton's career in the Senate: She wouldn't be where she was without her celebrity. And she couldn't survive there if she acted like one. Even before she won her unlikely bid to be the junior senator from New York, it was clear she would be held to a different standard in the upper congressional chamber. On election night 2000, Republican majority leader Trent Lott told the national press as Clinton rolled to victory, "I'll tell you one thing: when this Hillary gets to the Senate, if she does—maybe lightning will strike and she won't—she will be one of 100, and we won't let her forget it." To survive in the Senate, a body known for its members jockeying for higher office, she'd need to be extraordinarily ordinary.

When Hillary Clinton and John McCain posed together along the red carpet at the premiere of the World War II action film

VISITING THE TROOPS *The freshman senator toured U.S. barracks in Iraq in Nov. 2003.*

The Great Raid in the muggy D.C. summer of 2005, movie mogul Harvey Weinstein jokingly introduced the pair as "the first great 2008 bipartisan presidential ticket." But the pair was united by more than shared Oval Office ambitions—they had become genuinely close, due in no small part to Clinton's hard work.

Throughout her Senate career, Clinton worked tirelessly to cultivate relationships with the GOP, including some of the same lawmakers who had brought articles of impeachment against her husband. It was the result of a carefully calibrated, and above all cautious, strategy that Clinton adopted to make the most of being one of 100. Too visible and she'd attract media hordes. Too partisan, and she'd poison her future ambitions. At Whitehaven, the Washington mansion she and Bill bought for $3 million

with the help of the advance for her memoir *Living History*, Clinton created a salon-like environment for her colleagues, donors and the Washington establishment.

Early on, Clinton was fastidious about attending hearings and votes, missing just five roll calls in her first two years in office, among the best record of any lawmaker. She would cancel events, meetings, and even Passover seders with supporters when votes got in the way. Wary of upsetting more-senior Senate colleagues, she showed up at hearings early, even though her newcomer status meant she would be among the last to speak. The press, especially the New York tabloids, noticed her every move. Clinton fumed when a *Washington Post* gossip column ran a photo of her at a hearing where she wasn't wearing makeup, writing that her "dry-and-go bangs hang limply down her forehead like rain-battered weeds." But Clinton was there—and always fully prepared.

The gossip-column incident reinforced Clinton's legendary contempt for the press, going back to the White House scandals. On the campaign trail, Clinton notoriously ignored her traveling press corps. In the halls of Congress, where it's common for camera-hungry lawmakers to pause to offer their perspectives on the news of the day, Clinton would duck the other way, and often for good reason. She was dogged by lingering questions over her husband's final pardons as he left office the same month she was sworn in, Jan. 2001. When it was alleged that her brother Hugh Rodham took $400,000 for "legal services" for a commutation of a Los Angeles drug dealer and a Florida fraudster, Clinton denied knowledge and said she was "extremely disappointed in this terrible misjudgment that he made." Clinton herself had attended a meeting with her husband and the grand rabbi of an upstate New York Hasidic sect seeking commutations for four associates. The Skver sect delivered nearly 1,400 votes for Clinton and just 12 for Lazio. Weeks later, President Clinton awarded the commutations, though the senator denied she'd ever discussed the matter with him.

Seeking to sidestep the drama, Clinton threw herself into the behind-the-scenes monotony of Capitol Hill, from the weekly Democratic caucus luncheons to Wednesday prayer breakfasts hosted by the Christian group The Fellowship. In one meeting, Kansas firebrand Sam Brownback pleaded with Clinton to forgive him for hurtful things he had said about her when she was First Lady. She did, building yet another across-the-aisle working friendship.

She worked with former House speaker Newt Gingrich on a health-care initiative. Senate majority leader Bill Frist partnered with her on digital-medical-records legislation. With Brownback she co-sponsored a measure protecting refugees fleeing sexual abuse. And even Lott came around to work with her on improving the Federal Emergency Management Agency. Working to burnish her family-values credentials, Clinton introduced the Family Entertainment Protection Act to impose fines for selling mature-rated video games to minors, along with a measure to ban flag burning.

Those efforts rarely progressed beyond committee, let alone became law. Clinton was a prolific bill sponsor, putting her name behind 417 bills in her eight-year Senate career, of which just three were signed into law. But colleagues on both sides coveted her backing and lauded her work, with the Clinton name instantly elevating an ordinary bill into a national story. Despite voting overwhelmingly with her party on key votes, Clinton's reach across the aisle enabled her to cast herself as a centrist lawmaker ready to win a general election.

South Carolina conservative senator Lindsey Graham, one of the managers of Bill Clinton's impeachment when he was a House member, praised Clinton in TIME for building bridges. "In the Senate, a small body of big egos, Senator Clinton is sought out by her colleagues to form legislative partnerships," he wrote. "Her high-profile status, combined with a reputation as a smart, prepared, serious senator, creates real influence."

On the morning of Sept. 11, 2001, Hillary Clinton heard about a lone plane crashing into the World Trade Center's north tower before she left her home for the Capitol. Sitting in the back of her car, Clinton heard a radio report that the south tower had also been hit, realizing at that moment, as the rest of America did, that it was no accident. But unlike most Americans, Clinton was in a position to do something about it. Before she could talk with Chelsea, whose cell phone was unreachable on the jammed

BIPARTISAN BUDDIES
Presidential challengers Clinton and McCain, here at the 2007 National Prayer Breakfast in Washington, became unlikely allies in the Senate.

Manhattan networks, Clinton spoke with her husband, who was in Australia preparing to deliver a speech, telling him with little evidence, "Everything's fine, don't worry."

Clinton made it to the Capitol, only to be evacuated to the headquarters building of the Capitol Police, where she finally got through to her daughter. She spoke again with the former president, telling him Chelsea was out of harm's way. The pair spoke frequently, "quite often, all night long," as Bill Clinton told a reporter days after the attacks, discussing the recovery and the nation's response to the terror attack. She appeared live on CNN that night minutes before President George W. Bush addressed the nation, a changed Hillary's first public appearance to a changed nation.

When she first took office, Clinton secured seats for herself on committees dealing with health, education and the environment, gushing in a press release that it would allow her to "continue the work I have been doing for over 30 years on behalf of children and families." Suddenly those assignments seemed less relevant. "That September morning changed me and what I had to do as a senator, a New Yorker, and an American," she wrote in her memoir.

In short order, Clinton backed the invasion of Afghanistan and the Patriot Act. She worked to procure funding to rebuild downtown New York. Exercising the classic strategy of political triangulation, Clinton was a vocal critic of the Bush administration for failing to investigate the environmental conditions near Ground Zero, earning her points with the Democratic base. And then, fatefully, she voted in favor of the 2002 Iraq war resolution.

"Perhaps my decision is influenced by my eight years of experience on the other end of Pennsylvania Avenue, in the White House, watching my husband deal with serious challenges to our nation," Clinton said, by way of explaining her vote on the Senate floor. The votes were an extension of Clinton's long-standing hawkish foreign policy, tracing to her support for humanitarian interventions during her time in the White House, and in line with her future ambitions.

Already strategizing a presidential campaign, both Clintons knew she needed to portray a face of steely resolve if she was to be the first female commander in chief. "We will also stand united behind our president as he and his advisers plan the necessary actions to demonstrate America's resolve and commitment," she said from the Senate floor the day after the attacks. "Not only to seek out and exact punishment on the perpetrators, but to make very clear that not only those who harbor terrorists, but those who in any way aid or comfort them whatsoever, will now face the wrath of our country."

Clinton obtained a spot on the Senate Armed Services Committee—the first New Yorker ever to serve on the committee. She cozied up to the nation's military brass, overcoming their skepticism about her with robust preparation and support for their priorities. She was among the first lawmakers to highlight the need for improved armor for American troops fighting in Iraq, drawing praise from the Pentagon.

Clinton not only voted to authorize a strike on Iraq but voted against an amendment pushed by senator Carl Levin to require the Bush administration to try first to build a U.N. coalition for the attack and, failing that, to come back to Congress for a direct vote on a unilateral strike. She was one of the few Democrats to repeat the Bush administration's later discredited—and at the time disputed—assertion that Saddam Hussein was in cahoots with al-Qaeda. Senator Joe Biden, who voted for the war resolution, debunked the al-Qaeda connection in his remarks on the Senate floor.

LIVELY EXCHANGE *Clinton sidebars with senior Senate partner Chuck Schumer in May 2001.*

Clinton appears never to have read the full National Intelligence Estimate used by the Bush administration to justify the war but said she was briefed on its contents. That report gave at least some of her colleagues pause, with Florida Democrat and Intelligence Committee chair Bob Graham citing it as unpersuasive in showing that Hussein possessed weapons of mass destruction.

Clinton never apologized for the vote, even as it became a serious handicap during her race for the Democratic presidential nomination. "I take responsibility for my vote, and I, along with a majority of Americans, expect the president and his administration to take responsibility for the false assurances, faulty evidence and mismanagement of the war," she wrote in an email to constituents in late 2005. She said she felt misled after Bush administration officials "publicly and privately assured me" that they

would try to avoid war. As the Democratic Party's support for the war faded, Clinton opposed the Bush administration's surge, but she also refused to endorse dramatic troop-withdrawal plans pushed by other members of her party, including Obama. "I reject a rigid timetable that the terrorists can exploit," she told a group of Kentucky Democrats in 2005, "and I reject an open timetable that has no ending attached to it."

The shadow of the Iraq vote would prove to be too long for her to outrun in 2008. The root of defeat, in fact, may have been Clinton abandoning the understated approach that allowed her to break out in her own right in the Senate. The traditions of the Senate—and her ability to embrace them—helped bring about one of the greatest political rehabilitations in American history, turning a polarizing First Lady into an inevitable presidential nominee.

A FIRST BID FOR PRESIDENT

SHE ENTERED THE 2008 RACE WITH
EVERY ADVANTAGE. WHAT WENT WRONG?
BY JAY NEWTON-SMALL

BATTLEFIELD IOWA
"Just call me Hillary" in
Waterloo on July 4, 2007

"I announced today that I'm forming a presidential exploratory committee," Hillary Clinton said, sitting in a red jacket on a sofa in her home, soft yellow lamplight behind her. The welcoming scene, practically inviting viewers to sit down and have tea, belied the import of the video: with those words on Jan. 20, 2007, Clinton made her historic bid for the presidency official.

Her declaration marked a bunch of firsts. She was the first former First Lady to seek the presidency and the first woman to enter the race as the front-runner. If elected, she would become the first female president, making Bill Clinton the first First Husband.

Tellingly, Clinton remarked on none of these glass ceilings in her announcement. From the start, she downplayed the historic nature of her candidacy, portraying herself as no different or less tough than her male colleagues. She presented herself as personally conservative, even stolid; someone not prone to histrionics. And then there was the Clinton machine, steeped in polling

and focus groups, powerful fundraisers and a massive top-down operation. She entered the race with the force of a hurricane, absorbing tens of millions of dollars in donations, drawing crowds in the thousands wherever she went. The nomination was hers to lose.

Clinton's name recognition was both a blessing and a curse. Everyone in America knew who she was and had an opinion about her. In the summer of 2006, her staff pondered how to get around the baggage that came with her fame. Mark Penn, Clinton's pollster, argued that she should run as a "responsible progressive," a sober moderate appealing to a right-leaning center disgusted by George W. Bush. Without too serious a challenge from the left, staking out the middle ground would make the general-election pivot easy. Her staff agonized over how to refer to her. She wasn't Hillary Clinton, the cuckolded wife or the author of Hillarycare. Nor was she Mrs. Clinton, or Ms. Rodham Clinton. As all her signs declared, she was simply "Hillary."

Although Clinton began the campaign with a 54% approval rating, according to a *Washington Post*/ABC News poll, only 41% of Democrats said they supported her. Senate majority leader Harry Reid and New York senator Chuck Schumer, concerned that Clinton's candidacy would dredge up scandals from affairs to impeachment, approached freshman Illinois senator Barack Obama in the fall of 2006 about running for president. Few politicians inspired vitriol on the right like the Clintons, and they worried that Hillary might not be able to overcome what would assuredly be a nasty general election. They wanted to turn the page to

CENTER OF ATTENTION *The front-runner, she took most of the hits in a 2007 debate in South Carolina.*

the next generation. And Obama, who had spent less than two years in the Senate at the time, inspired hope and change.

Obama announced that he was forming an exploratory committee four days before Clinton's announcement. Clinton's staff, so focused on building her apparatus, did not see the Obama threat coming until it was almost too late. Clinton's carefully calibrated image had to be tweaked at the last minute. Her platform of experience needed to compete with Obama's message of change.

To Clinton's mind, she'd been at the forefront of political change her whole life. A classic representative of the baby boomer generation, she was the Goldwater Girl turned antiwar activist turned progressive Democrat. She was, as her Secret Service nickname, "Evergreen," suggested, everything old that was new again. "Hill-

ary brings a lifetime record of accomplishments to this campaign—and yes, some of them were during the '90s," Clinton's communications director Howard Wolfson told TIME. "We think voters are asking—at a time when every candidate is talking about change—who actually has a record of accomplishing it their entire adult life?"

A SHAKY START

Clinton's image was the first in a host of challenges, starting with her vote for the resolution authorizing President George W. Bush to go to war in Iraq—a war Obama had proudly opposed from the start. On Jan. 11, 2007, Clinton took a last trip abroad, going to Kuwait, Iraq, Afghanistan and Pakistan. Upon her return, she announced her support for a phased withdrawal from Iraq. "The president's team is

A FAMILY AFFAIR *Campaigning with daughter Chelsea and mother Dorothy Rodham (right), Dec. 2007*

pursuing a failed strategy in Iraq as it edges closer to collapse, and Afghanistan needs more of our concerted effort and attention," she said in a press conference. Three days later, on Jan. 20, she announced her candidacy, saying she would "bring the right end" to the war in Iraq—turning herself from a supporter of the Iraq war into one of its most vociferous opponents.

Her next challenge was money. Fresh from re-election to the Senate, Clinton ended 2006 with $11 million in the bank for a presidential run. But some of her campaign advisers worried that she had spent too much on getting re-elected—$41 million, to her opponent's $6 million—and might not have enough for 2008. They agreed that she had to come out of the gate

strong, to underline an air of inevitability. She made a huge push in the first quarter of 2007, raising $20 million for the primary, but was stunned when Obama revealed that he had raised $23.5 million in the same period. Obama beat Clinton again in the second quarter. But she clawed her way back, besting him in the last two quarters. In the end, however, Obama raised $98.5 million to fund his primary run, versus Clinton's $93 million.

Meanwhile, she was falling behind on the campaign trail. With just a month until the Iowa caucuses, Clinton had spent 52 days in the state, visiting just 38 of its 99 counties, compared with 68 visited by Obama. When polls after Thanksgiving showed a three-way tie between Obama,

Clinton and former North Carolina senator John Edwards, the campaign dispatched some 300 staffers to Iowa, and campaign manager Patti Solis Doyle moved there to oversee the operation. Clinton, her husband, daughter Chelsea and mother Dorothy spent the last three weeks of 2007 trudging through the Iowa slush and snow trying to shake as many hands as possible in a state where retail politics famously matters.

Clinton also struggled with her message. She had assembled a team of insiders who had spent years or even decades with the Clintons: Penn, ad maker Mandy Grunwald, policy adviser Neera Tanden, Solis Doyle, Wolfson and tactician Harold Ickes. To call them a team of rivals is an understatement. Some, including her husband, wanted Clinton to run on her experience; her slogan was "Ready to Lead from Day One." Others argued that made her the de facto incumbent at a time when the public was rejecting the status quo. The fight played out in newspaper stories and onstage. One week Clinton would campaign with luminaries from her husband's administration and, of course, her husband himself; the next, she'd share the stage with her daughter, pronouncing herself the true agent of change.

Just before Christmas 2007, the campaign rented the infamous Des Moines hall where Howard Dean's 2004 candidacy went down with a scream and invited volunteers, staff and media for a holiday party with the Clintons. But a week before the party, the campaign had to scale back the catering from more than 1,000 to a few hundred. They invited staff and volunteers from all eight Democratic candidates, hoping to fill the space. In the end, only a few dozen people showed up, mostly media and staff for New Mexico governor Bill Richardson. Neither Clinton attended, citing weather and scheduling conflicts.

THE COMEBACK KID

The party proved to be an ominous sign. On Jan. 3, 2008, Obama won Iowa with 38% of the vote, followed by Edwards with 29.8% and Clinton a close third, garnering 29.5%. Such a loss would have been fatal to most campaigns. But Clinton took it as a wake-up call. "This race begins tonight and ends when Democrats throughout America have their say," Solis Doyle said in a statement. "Our campaign was built for a marathon." Five days later was the New Hampshire primary, and the Granite State had a history of helping the Clintons come back from the dead. In 1992, New Hampshire picked Bill Clinton, helping him to resurrect his faltering campaign and declare himself the "comeback kid."

While Hillary hoped New Hampshire might grant her the same boon, her campaign was in a state of shock at her defeat in Iowa. Donors were panicking, and there was talk of a staff shake-up. A handful of Clinton's closest confidants gathered friends and allies in Washington and flew north. They began knocking on every Democratic door on Clinton's lists. Her first event in New Hampshire delivered another blow: at the Democratic Party's 100 Club dinner, Clinton was booed by a handful of supporters when she declared she was working on "change for you," while Obama was greeted like the conquering hero. His polling numbers in New Hampshire had shot up 10 points after his surprise win in Iowa.

But an Obama misstep and an unguarded moment on a campaign stop gave Clinton her comeback. During a debate at St. Anselm College in Manchester, a moderator asked Clinton what she'd tell voters who were hesitant to vote for her "on the likability issue, where they seem to like Barack Obama more."

"Well, that hurts my feelings," Clinton said with a smile. Without looking up from

ADORING CROWDS
Even when she lagged in the polls in early 2008, Hillary still drew 4,000 to Minneapolis's Augsburg College.

his podium, Obama slyly quipped, "You're likable enough, Hillary."

Obama's appeal with women voters plummeted, as critics accused him of condescension. Then, two days later, an exhausted Clinton teared up during a stop at a Portsmouth coffee shop. "I couldn't do it if I didn't just passionately believe it was the right thing to do," she told a mostly female audience, her voice breaking. "I have so many opportunities from this country, and I just don't want to see us fall backwards as a nation. This is very personal for me." After nearly a year of stiff speeches and the avoidance of any emotion, the raw moment went viral. Two days later, on the back of overwhelming female support, Clinton won a surprise 3% victory over Obama in New Hampshire. She was still in it to win it.

She went on to win the Nevada caucuses, but Obama won South Carolina, sending him into Super Tuesday with 63 pledged delegates to Clinton's 48. At stake were 23 states and territories, accounting for 1,681 delegates. To cinch the nomination, a candidate needed 2,117 delegates. Obama focused on keeping the race close in big states like California and investing in smaller states with rich delegate counts. Obama's strategy worked: on Super Tuesday, he bested Clinton with 13 states and 847 delegates—even though Clinton won 50.2% of all votes cast.

By this time, the Democratic establishment had begun to break ranks. On Jan. 10, 2008, former presidential nominee Massachusetts senator John Kerry endorsed Obama. Three days later, Missouri senator Claire McCaskill, who was a fan of the Clintons but once said she wouldn't "want my daughter near" Bill Clinton, also came out in support of Obama. But the biggest blow came eight days before Super Tuesday when Massachusetts senator Teddy Kennedy risked the Clintons' wrath to endorse

Obama. Less than a week later, his niece, California First Lady Maria Shriver, followed suit.

The day after Super Tuesday, Clinton announced that she'd been forced to personally loan her campaign $5 million in February. The news came in contrast to Obama's record haul in January of $32 million. On Feb. 10, facing a long month of caucuses and primaries in heavily African American states, where Obama looked likely to win, Clinton shook up her staff, firing campaign manager Solis Doyle and replacing her with Maggie Williams. But by the end of February, Clinton was trailing Obama by more than 100 delegates—a seemingly insurmountable lead—and her cash was dwindling. Obama's momentum, and savvy strategy, had won him millions of small-dollar donors, while most of Clinton's large-dollar donors had already maxed out and could give no more. Clinton staked everything on March 4, dubbed "mini–Super Tuesday," with four states and 370 delegates at stake. Yet again she defied the odds.

Ohio and Texas were big states that played to Clinton's strengths: white, older and Latino voters. Polls in mid-February showed her leading in Texas by 10 percentage points and in Ohio by 20. Shedding her stiffness, Clinton went on *Saturday Night Live* and mocked the media for being too in love with Obama. The campaign also launched an effective television ad questioning Obama's preparedness to handle a foreign crisis. "It's 3 a.m., and your children are safe and asleep," but in a "dangerous world," the ad asked viewers, "who do you want answering the phone?"

Clinton won Ohio decisively. She also won the Texas primary, though she lost the Texas caucuses. In her victory speech, she declared herself the comeback kid. "For everyone here in Ohio and across America who's ever been counted out but refused to

TWO FOR ONE *Bill (in Iowa in 2007) proved both an asset and a liability to Hillary's campaign.*

be knocked out, and for everyone who has stumbled but stood right back up, and for everyone who works hard and never gives up, this one is for you," she told a roaring audience in Columbus, Ohio.

Clinton won Pennsylvania in April but lost North Carolina in May. She won Indiana, but only by 2 percentage points, essentially splitting the delegates with Obama yet again. By this time, Obama was leading by more than 150 delegates. With few primaries left, Clinton's path to the nomination had significantly narrowed. One way she could win was if all of the superdelegates, about 800 elected officials and party leaders—roughly 20% of the total 4,233 delegates—swung her way. By April, however, Democratic leaders such as House speaker Nancy Pelosi had publicly said it would be damaging for superdelegates to overturn the

will of the people, effectively cutting off that path for Clinton. The other route hinged on a May 31 meeting of the obscure Democratic National Committee's Rules and Bylaws Committee meeting. Both Michigan and Florida had broken the DNC's rules and moved moved their primaries ahead in the calendar in the hopes of playing a pivotal role in the election. Well before any votes were cast, the DNC punished both states by stripping them of their combined 313 pledged delegates. All the candidates had agreed not to campaign in either state, and Obama wasn't even on the Michigan ballot. Clinton had won both contests handily and by the end of May was calling on the DNC to seat all her delegates, which would have helped her catch up to Obama.

In a dramatic nine-hour meeting at the Marriott Wardman Park hotel in Wash-

ington, the committee voted unanimously
to count half of Florida's delegates and to
split Michigan's delegates 69 for Clinton,
59 for Obama, though he wasn't even on
the Michigan ballot. The result netted
Clinton 24 delegates, but Obama still led
by 137 delegates. Outraged, Clinton supporters in the room chanted "McCain '08!"
Ickes, who represented Clinton at the meeting, accused the committee of "hijacking"
the election and called the decision
"a perversion."

On June 1, Clinton won the Puerto Rico
primary in a landslide. But two days later,
on the day of the South Dakota and Montana primaries, Obama announced the
endorsement of 28 superdelegates, putting
him over the 2,117 delegates needed to
secure the nomination. That night, Clinton
won the South Dakota primary but lost
Montana. At a victory party in the base-
ment of Yeshiva University in her home
state of New York, Clinton doggedly refused to concede. Four days later, she finally
endorsed Obama at a rally at the National
Building Museum in Washington.

Ultimately, Clinton garnered 17,857,501
million votes, the most of any women to
run for any U.S. office ever. "Although we
weren't able to shatter that highest, hardest
glass ceiling this time, thanks to you, it's
got about 18 million cracks in it, and the
light is shining through like never before,
filling us all with the hope and the sure
knowledge that the path will be a little
easier next time," Clinton said.

Clinton exited the race with a 58% approval rating. She had succeeded in redefin-
ing herself, overcoming her own stereotype
and caricature. She had proven that a
female candidate could be just as tough as
a male candidate and still show emotion.
To that end, she cracked the glass ceiling
for the next female candidate for president,
whether it's her or someone else.

HILLARY CONCEDES
Before a teary crowd of thousands at Washington's National Building Museum on June 7, 2008, she ends her 16-month campaign.

CIRCLING A TROUBLED GLOBE

AS SECRETARY OF STATE, HILLARY SOUGHT TO MANAGE CONFLICT, WHICH SOMETIMES INCLUDED GETTING SINGED HERSELF BY MASSIMO CALABRESI

SETTING THE STAGE
Secretary of State Clinton (in March 2011 with aide Huma Abedin, foreground) heads for a congressional hearing on severing ties with Libya.

In the early days of the Republic, being secretary of state was a powerful credential for an American politician: from 1801 to 1841, every president but Andrew Jackson had previously served as top diplomat for the young country. But not since James Buchanan disastrously set the stage for the Civil War has a former secretary of state occupied the White House. In late 2008, as she weighed president-elect Barack Obama's offer to become the country's 67th secretary of state, Hillary Clinton was surely aware of the challenges, and perhaps also the advantages, that accepting the job would bring should she ever decide to run for president again.

Foreign policy had already played an unhelpful role in her 2008 Democratic primary loss. Obama ran hard to Clinton's left on national security that year, targeting her 2002 vote in favor of authorizing the Bush administration's use of military force against Iraq. It proved a highly effective maneuver; the party's left wing aligned behind Obama early, and Clinton never caught up.

If it was true that Clinton was more

10-YEAR HUNT ENDS *President Obama and key staff watch Navy SEALs close in on Osama bin Laden in 2011. "Those were the most intense 38 minutes," Clinton said of the raid that killed bin Laden.*

BETTER DAYS *President Putin warmly welcomes Clinton to a Sept. 2012 summit in Russia.*

hawkish than Obama, the prospect of being his secretary of state also meant she wouldn't have much room to disagree. But for Clinton, the advantages of taking the job were self-evident. After a bitter primary battle, her willingness not just to support Obama, but ultimately to accept him as her boss, highlighted her reputation inside the Democratic Party as a team player. It would give her virtually unmatched diplomatic credentials for any elected official not only in her party but in any party—an invaluable notch in any presidential candidate's belt. Most important, it was a job that interested her. Clinton as First Lady had emerged as a global player by embracing women's issues at a conference in Beijing in 1995, declaring in a speech that "human rights are women's rights and women's rights are human rights, once and for

all." From Foggy Bottom, she would be able to pursue that and other causes with force and with power. As a member of the Armed Services Committee in the Senate, Clinton had learned the nuts and bolts of national security, earning the respect of the military in the process and getting a taste for policymaking. From counterterrorism to great-power politics, Clinton had ideas about America's future abroad.

"All power has limits," Clinton said in an interview with TIME a few years into her tenure. "In a much more networked and multipolar world," she said, "we can't wave a magic wand and say to China or Brazil or India, 'Quit growing. Quit using your economies to assert power' . . . It's up to us to figure out how we position ourselves to be as effective as possible at different times in the face of different threats and opportunities."

SECURITY TALKS *Clinton meets with Saudi and Kuwaiti foreign ministers six months earlier.*

THE SEARCH FOR SMART POWER

When Clinton took the reins at State, she viewed what she called "convening power" as the key to rebuilding U.S. influence overseas after the sometimes tense years during the George W. Bush presidency: "One of the big questions that I certainly faced becoming secretary of state is, O.K., we're ready to lead. Are there others ready to be there on whatever agenda we are seeking? There was a lot of broken pottery, so to speak, in our relationships." That convening power was in turn part of what Clinton called smart power—the use of everything from public diplomacy and new media to development aid and public-private collaboration to protect and advance U.S. interests abroad in ways America's military power cannot.

Clinton pushed State to collaborate with nongovernment groups, which was some-

thing of a departure from past practice. She formed joint ventures with countless organizations, funding 67 programs dedicated to the rights of women, which offered a new flank against traditional forms of repression overseas and a cost-effective way to promote both security and development. The guiding national-security principle of the early Bush administration was that too much international cooperation weakens America, but Clinton found supporters in both parties who said that boosting cooperation produced results.

In some respects, America's limited power abroad mirrored Clinton's predicament as secretary of state. Though Obama practically begged her to become his top diplomat after the 2008 campaign, the job came with many strings attached. The White House handpicked her deputy and

ALL EYES ON SYRIA
Clinton (in Paris in 2012) joins the chorus of world leaders calling for the ouster of Syrian president Bashar Assad.

RECONNECTING *The former secretary of state visits the president in July 2013.*

quietly vetoed other appointments she wanted to make. While Clinton worked to build a relationship with her former adversary in the West Wing, her chief of staff, Cheryl Mills, played bad cop, having "tough conversations," according to one official, with deputy national-security adviser Denis McDonough over appointments and locking horns with the Treasury Department. Tension between the State Department and the National Security Council (NSC) continued throughout Clinton's time as top diplomat.

On policy, Clinton spoke out at key meetings, but on some big decisions, such as abandoning the push to close Guantánamo Bay, limiting the size of the Afghanistan troop surge and demanding that Israel stop settlement activity, Obama made the final call without her. Clinton's voice was heard:

she met weekly with Obama one on one and also weekly with his national-security adviser and secretary of defense. And in daily, formal NSC meetings, she made her arguments. But many of the final debates in the Obama administration were held in small rooms among Obama's closest White House aides—which Clinton, with her famously tight inner circle, could appreciate.

Clinton sought other avenues of influence, working to bolster her department's clout, expanding control over U.S. foreign-aid strategy and finding new sources of funding for it in the Pentagon's deep pockets. She also lashed her bureaucracy to more-powerful ones, boosting the number of her political advisers at the Defense Department from 15 to 100 in an attempt to steer Pentagon policy to State's benefit. In both instances, it helped that in defense secretary Robert Gates, Clinton had a partner in trying to build up State's role in national security. The two found common cause on the size and duration of the Afghanistan surge and on not releasing photos of the dead Osama bin Laden.

Abroad, Clinton worked to broker the marriage of diplomacy and technology. She boosted State's budget to pay for computer training and surveillance-evading software for dissidents, some of it top secret, from $15 million to $45 million. State Department officials claimed that the Syrian revolution continued in part because of a sanctions waiver for surveillance-evading software Clinton sought and won despite resistance from other agencies in 2009.

Whereas U.S. envoys once filed secret cables to Washington late at night, Clinton pushed her ambassadors to expand the use of Twitter and Facebook. (Her daughter, Chelsea, came to call her TechnoMom.) "We are in the age of participation," Clinton said at her husband's charity event in New York City in Sept. 2011, "and the challenge ... is to figure out how to be responsive, to help catalyze, unleash, channel the kind of participatory eagerness that is there."

Clinton tried to ensure that the changes she had introduced would be permanent:

SHE GAINED A PRIVATE CHEERING SECTION WITHIN THE CENTRIST WING THAT DOMINATED THE FOREIGN POLICY OF GEORGE H.W. BUSH.

she required every diplomat who rotated through the foreign-service institute to get training in social media. But most of her novel initiatives were run out of her office, giving them clout but leaving their survival to the discretion of her successor. Some, especially those with little or no independent budget, now face an uncertain future.

Clinton touted development as a tool of national strategy, spending $8 billion in 2010 on global health and boosting public-diplomacy funds for the U.S. embassy in Pakistan from $2 million to $50 million to get recognition for the billions in aid the U.S. has spent there. But foreign-aid successes in places like Afghanistan were mixed at best. Though he was a vocal supporter of Clinton, Vermont Democratic senator Patrick Leahy, who chaired the Appropriations Subcommittee on Foreign Operations, said of her handling of the issue, "Development projects have been launched on a scale that cannot possibly be sustained ... They have had to continually adjust goals and revise strategy and redefine what success is."

Clinton got good marks on her traditional diplomacy. At a July 2010 meeting in Hanoi of the Association of Southeast Asian Nations, which the U.S. had just joined, Clinton bluntly pushed back against China's newly expansionist rhetoric about the oil- and gas-rich South China Sea, over objections from senior aides like the late Richard Holbrooke. The result, say China experts, was a newly energized coalition against Chinese territorial aims in the region.

Both for her handling of relations with Russia, which yielded support for Iran sanctions and Russia's abstention during the U.N. vote authorizing the Libya mission, and her measured resistance on China, she gained a private cheering section within the centrist wing that dominated the foreign policy of George H.W. Bush. "She's been a good secretary of state," said the dean of American diplomacy, Brent Scowcroft, the first President Bush's national-security adviser. "She is confident but not arrogant in her confidence, and quite agile."

Clinton also relied on her legendary endurance. She maintained punishing 18-plus-hour-a-day schedules in her travels. During the U.N. General Assembly in New York in Sept. 2011, at the end of an endless day of one-on-one meetings, public appearances and forums, Clinton sat down in a closed session with the 27 European Union foreign ministers and listened and responded as each aired opinions on U.S. foreign policy, even as glazed looks settled over her staff. Late in her tenure, however, she and her aides got a reminder that she was not unstoppable. In Dec. 2012 Clinton caught a stomach virus, became severely dehydrated, and suffered a concussion when she fainted and fell. Her husband later said it took her six months to fully recover.

THE LIBYA TEST

The highest-profile test of Clinton's effort to mix her "smart power" approach with traditional tools would also prove her most politically controversial moment at the State Department. It came in Libya in the wake of the Arab Spring uprisings in 2011. With the country rising up against him, Libyan dictator Muammar Gaddafi threatened to kill citizens in retaliation, and Clinton saw a chance to demonstrate that the U.S. could form coalitions with new allies. It began with Clinton leading the behind-the-scenes effort that ended in Gaddafi's death, pushing wary neighbors to assist the rebels in their revolt. On March 12, 2011, the Arab League asked the U.N. to impose a no-fly zone, knowing that only the U.S. could lead such an operation. Clinton told the Arabs a U.S.-led no-fly zone alone wouldn't protect the civilians it was designed to help and instead worked to persuade the Qataris, Emiratis and Jordanians to join with the U.S. in striking Gaddafi's forces on the ground.

Success at that gave Clinton a shot at overcoming Russia's traditional reflexive veto of any U.N. resolution authorizing U.S.-led military intervention. Though Russia has its own restive minorities and fears broadly used American military might, Clinton told Obama she thought she could turn Russia around, with Arab countries asking for help and joining the fight. "Let's test that," Obama replied. And so, while traveling in Tunisia in March, Clinton placed a 15-minute call to Russian foreign minister Sergei Lavrov and persuaded him to abstain on a U.N. resolution authorizing direct strikes against Gaddafi's forces. "C'mon, Sergei, this is important, and the Arab League and the Arab countries are behind us," Clinton recalls telling Lavrov during the call.

Lavrov's O.K. cleared the way for Obama to launch more than 200 Tomahawk missiles against Libyan positions and provide the command and control for French, British and a handful of Arab fighters. But neither the traditional diplomacy at the U.N. nor the hard-power use of force

THE CONFLICT IN LIBYA AND ITS AFTERMATH WOULD PROVE TO BE HER MOST POLITICALLY CONTROVERSIAL MOMENT AT THE STATE DEPARTMENT.

HOT SEAT *Clinton testifies about the Benghazi consulate attack before a Senate panel in 2013.*

led to the immediate ouster of Gaddafi. So Clinton paired the high-level diplomacy with behind-the-scenes efforts to bolster anti-Gaddafi rebels. In Libya in July 2011, the rebels had salvaged telecommunications equipment from retreating Gaddafi forces in the eastern part of the country but could make only local calls and had no Internet access. State quietly helped restore full services beyond Gaddafi's control and got access to fiber-optic-cable networks that didn't run through Tripoli, allowing the rebels to gin up cash from abroad.

The behind-the-scenes work intensified after Gaddafi fled Tripoli. A little after noon on Sept. 22, 2011, Clinton arrived at the offices of the Qatari mission to the U.N. overlooking New York City's East River for a meeting with the Qatari Emir, Sheik Hamad bin Khalifa al-Thani. Al-Thani,

the burly, independent-minded patron of al-Jazeera who ousted his father in a 1995 coup, was a crucial Arab representative in the coalition Clinton assembled to go to war in Libya. He was also a deeply influential backer of several of the Libyan rebel figures who ousted Gaddafi from Tripoli. Clinton, worried that rebels would turn on one another and push Libya into chaos, urged al-Thani to encourage the rebel militias to unify.

Al-Thani said he'd do his best. But he worried that other allies' support for the struggling rebel leadership might flag with Tripoli having fallen—and that Gaddafi might launch a counterattack. He asked Clinton to convene the allies later in the day for an emergency meeting. By 5:30 p.m., Clinton's staff had brought representatives of the U.K., France, Italy, Qatar, Jordan and

DIPLOMATIC MISFIRE
Secretary Clinton's July 2012 Cairo visit was thwarted by power struggles between the president, Mohamed Morsi, the military and a deeply divided Egyptian populace.

other countries together in her suite on the 34th floor of the Waldorf-Astoria hotel a few blocks away. Clinton, who purposefully mixed a politician's cheerful warmth with a lawyer's face-the-facts arguments, harangued them to step up to the plate. The situation in Libya "could spin out of control very quickly," she told the diplomats, who wound up pledging continued attacks against loyalist forces and renewed support for the rebel leadership.

It would not be long before the dangers of rebel disunity became apparent. Less than a year later, on Sept. 11, 2012, the 11th anniversary of the 9/11 attacks, Islamic militants stormed two U.S. buildings in the eastern Libyan city of Benghazi, killing four Americans, including ambassador Chris Stevens. The catastrophic attack cast America's involvement in the chaotic Libyan uprising in a different light—and cast a shadow over Clinton's tenure as secretary of state, spawning fevered Republican accusations of incompetence and of a Clinton-led cover-up. Several high-level commissions found senior officials at the State Department at fault for failing to provide sufficient security for the U.S. facilities in Benghazi, though none have blamed Clinton herself.

Libya itself remains a largely ungoverned mess. Tribes and other armed factions have seized oil production facilities, crippling the economy's energy sector. Public outrage has forced the dissolution of parliament and early elections. Nevertheless, the U.S. has had some successes there. On Oct. 5, 2013, the U.S. collaborated with local Libyan officials to detain Anas al-Libi, an alleged member of al-Qaeda wanted for the 1998 bombing of the U.S. embassies in Kenya and Tanzania.

The larger question is whether, as secretary of state, Clinton succeeded in mixing new and old techniques to advance American interests. The Libyan uprising was just one of many rebellions that formed the Arab Spring revolts against dictators across the Middle East, several of which continue to spread unrest. Clinton argued that in a world where borders and government were becoming less important, the U.S. needed to side with the rebellions, and she actively sought to use the "smart power" tools of technology to advance their causes.

"As we look at how we manage the Arab Spring," Clinton told TIME in 2011, "we are trying to influence the direction, with full recognition that we don't have ownership and we don't have control. And there's a lot that's going to happen that is unpredictable. But we want to lead by our values and our interests in ways that, regardless of the trajectory over the next decade, people will know the United States was on the side of democracy, on the side of the rule of law . . . And that will, I hope, be a strong antidote to the voices of either fatalism or extremism."

When Clinton left State, the public, at least, was giving her high marks. A picture by TIME's Diana Walker of Hillary reading her smartphone aboard a military aircraft en route to Libya in 2011 went viral and then became a meme about women in power. The controversy over Benghazi also persisted, and remained a cloud over her tenure, but ultimately Clinton's time at the State Department had worked in her favor. She had cemented her reputation as a competent figure on the international stage and earned the near-endorsement of that stalwart Republican realist Robert Gates. With Osama bin Laden dead, the wars in Iraq and Afghanistan nearly over, and the Republican Party relitigating its longtime ideological divide between isolationists and traditional hawks, Clinton was well positioned if, as many expected her to, she chose once again to apply for the job of commander in chief.

/14/92

5/10/93

3/21/94

/31/98

2/22/99

3/1/99

3/17/08

5/5/08

2/18/08

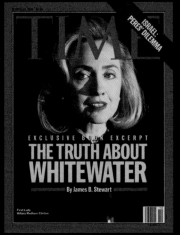

3/18/96

7/1/96

10/20/97

6/16/03

8/28/06

11/19/07

11/16/09

11/7/11

1/27/14

ANCHORED BY FAITH

SINCE CHILDHOOD, HILLARY'S
METHODIST BELIEFS HAVE INSPIRED
PUBLIC SERVICE AND PRIVATE
DEVOTION BY ELIZABETH DIAS

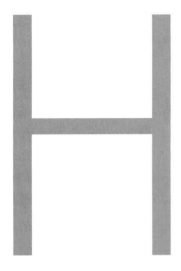

Hillary Clinton once described her faith as the background music of her life. Whether she hears it as Chopin, Bach or even U2, she did not say, but the tune, she said, never fades away. "It's there all the time. It's not something you have to think about, you believe it," she said in an interview with the *New York Times*. "You have a faith center out of which the rest flows."

It can be easy to tune out background music, especially amid the political cacophony that has so often dominated Clinton's public life. But the former secretary of state, U.S. senator and First Lady is, and has always been, a Methodist. Her faith is at once public yet personal, quiet yet bold. She is part of the second-largest Protestant group in the country, but her brand of faith has never been mainstream: Methodists make up about 6% of the total U.S. adult population, according to the Pew Research Center.

If Methodists are known for one thing, it is, as the old church saying goes, that they are always looking for a mission. Clinton

is no exception. Her sense of purpose has guided her from Wellesley to Washington, and may push her to seek the White House again come 2016. Certainly political aspirations have motivated her career. But her faith has also driven her, if not equally, at least consistently, to give her life to the pursuit of a higher calling.

STEP BY STEP

Methodism knew Clinton even before she was born. Family lore has it that John Wesley, the founder of the Methodist Church, converted her great-great-grandparents in the coal-mining villages of Newcastle, in northeast England, in the 19th century. Clinton grew up attending First United Methodist Church of Park Ridge in Chicago, where she was confirmed in sixth grade. Her mother taught Sunday school, and Clinton was active in youth group, Bible studies and altar guild. On Saturdays during Illinois's harvest season, she and others from her youth group would babysit children of nearby migrant workers. As the Wesleyan mantra instructed them, "Do all the good you can, by all the means you can, in all the ways you can, in all the places you can, at all the times you can, to all the people you can, as long as ever you can."

One man in particular had a strong influence on her young faith: Donald Jones, who came to Park Ridge as the new youth minister when Clinton was a high school freshman. A Drew University Seminary graduate, Jones's own theology had the imprint of theological heavyweights like Dietrich Bonhoeffer and Reinhold Niebuhr, and he made it his mission to give the youth a strong and broad theological training. He

TIES THAT BIND *Hillary, a deeply committed Methodist, and Bill, a Southern Baptist, sing together in 1978, most likely in Hillary's Little Rock church.*

SPIRITUAL MENTOR *The late Rev. Donald Jones (in 2007) taught Hillary about social justice.*

created a "University of Life" for his youth-group students and introduced Clinton and her peers to the great works of T.S. Eliot, E.E. Cummings, Dostoyevsky and Picasso. Faith, he argued, must be lived out in social justice and human rights. Jones ensured that students connected these ideas to life in their own communities, arranging exchanges with youth groups at black and Hispanic churches in Chicago's inner city so that his students became aware of life beyond Park Ridge. Most important, he introduced Clinton to Martin Luther King Jr. when he came to Chicago in 1962. "Until then, I had been dimly aware of the social revolution occurring in our country," Clinton recalled in her memoir *Living History*, "but Dr. King's words illuminated the struggle taking place and challenged our indifference."

This socially active current remained the lifeblood of her faith as her political career began to take shape. At Wellesley, Clinton regularly read the Methodist Church's *Motive* magazine, and she credited it with helping her to realize that her political beliefs were no longer aligned with the Republican Party and that she should step down as president of the Young Republicans. During her Yale Law School years, she worked for anti-poverty activist Marian Wright Edelman, who is now president of the Children's Defense Fund, and researched the education and health of migrant children she had known earlier. When she finally decided to marry a young Southern Baptist named Bill Clinton in Oct. 1975, it was local Arkansas Methodist minister Vic Nixon who married them in their living room.

Clinton became the first Methodist First

Lady in the White House since President Warren Harding's wife, Florence, who followed Methodist First Ladies Ida McKinley, Lucy Hayes, Julia Grant and Eliza Johnson. She soon brought issues like health-care reform and women's rights to the national spotlight (even though faith alone could not make what came to be known as "Hillarycare" succeed). The Clintons regularly attended the Foundry United Methodist Church, a socially active church that today is an advocate for gay and lesbian rights, not far from 1600 Pennsylvania Avenue. "As a Christian, part of my obligation is to take action to alleviate suffering," she told the United Methodist News Service not long after her husband was elected. "Explicit recognition of that in the Methodist tradition is one reason I'm comfortable in this church."

While Clinton's faith has always emphasized public service, it also has a private side that runs deep. Prayer and reflection have been at the core of her spiritual life, and she has been known to carry a small book of her favorite Scripture verses to reflect upon in quiet moments. "My faith has always been primarily personal," she once told the *New York Times*. "It is how I live my life and who I am, and I have tried through my works to demonstrate a level of commitment and compassion that flow from my faith."

At times, she would let the public catch a glimpse of this inner faith. When George

H.W. Bush called Bill on election night in 1992 to concede, Hillary recalled in *Living History*, "Bill and I went into our bedroom, closed the door and prayed together for God's help as he took on this awesome honor and responsibility." Her words are an unmistakable echo for anyone who knows the Bible well. Jesus, in his Sermon on the Mount, preached, "But whenever you pray, go into your room and shut the door and pray to your Father who is in secret; and your Father who sees in secret will reward you."

It is a reminder that Clinton is keenly aware that in America the Bible can often be a political tool. Early in 1993, she joined a women's prayer group through the National Prayer Breakfast organized by conservative evangelical Doug Coe. Clinton called the women her "prayer partners," in the long spiritual tradition of having people of faith pray consistently for you throughout your life. The group, however, was more than just spiritual—each woman had strong political affiliations, many of which served to help Clinton win allies across the political aisle. It included Susan Baker, the wife of President George H.W. Bush's secretary of state, James Baker; Joanne Kemp, the wife of future vice-presidential candidate Jack Kemp; and Holly Leachman, a Christian speaker who even faxed Clinton a daily Scripture reading or faith message throughout her time in the White House. Whether the group served a primarily political or spiritual purpose is difficult to sort out, but Clinton did say that she valued their prayers. "Of all the thousands of gifts I received in my eight years in the White House, few were more welcome and needed," she wrote.

Clinton had plenty of raw personal moments that thrust her faith into the public spotlight. Her second year in the White House was particularly grief-stricken: she lost her father, her mother-in-law and

METHODISTS, AS THE OLD CHURCH SAYING GOES, ARE ALWAYS LOOKING FOR A MISSION.

her friend Vince Foster in the short time since Bill Clinton had been president. Two friends gave Clinton a copy of a book by Catholic priest Henri Nouwen, *The Return of the Prodigal Son*. One sentence, Clinton said, struck her like a lightning bolt: "The discipline of gratitude is the explicit effort to acknowledge that all I am and have is given to me as a gift of love, a gift to be celebrated with joy."

The biggest test of faith came in 1998 with her husband's personal indiscretions. To the public, Clinton's response was short and direct. "This is a time when she relies on her strong religious faith," Marsha Berry, Clinton's press secretary, said in a statement when the Monica Lewinsky news broke. But as she often did in times of personal trial, Clinton turned back to her former minister Don Jones for counsel. He pointed her to a sermon by theologian Paul Tillich called "You Are Accepted" that he had taught her youth group growing up and encouraged her to choose grace. "Grace strikes us when we are in great pain and restlessness," Tillich wrote. "It happens or it does not happen." Clinton explained in her memoir that she made a decision to choose grace. She also turned to Nouwen for advice on forgiveness. Prayer, Nouwen argues, takes you into the arms of God and deep into yourself to find the ability to forgive. "Do I want to be not just the one who is being forgiven, but also the one who forgives; not just the one who is being welcomed home, but also the one who welcomes home; not just the one who receives compassion, but the one who offers it as well?" he reflected in his book's conclusion.

Clinton also developed a close relationship with evangelist Billy Graham in the months leading to and after the crisis. In 1997, at the dedication of the George Herbert Walker Bush Presidential Library, Clinton pulled Graham aside and asked him to

talk with her. "She grabbed my head in her hands and held it there like that and looked right into my eyes and said, 'I want to tell you about Bill,'" Graham later recounted in *The Preacher and the Presidents*. Graham, who forgave Bill Clinton as quickly as he had Nixon decades prior, encouraged Hillary to forgive her husband. Clinton held Graham's hand the entire time during their private meeting at Graham's New York City Crusade in 2005. "She was just so sweet," Graham recalled. "She is different from the Hillary you see in the media. There is a warm side to her—and a spiritual one."

COSTLY GRACE

There's a strain of Christian theology that believes self-sacrifice to be the highest form of faithful living. It was Dietrich Bonhoeffer who famously said that when Christ calls a man, he bids him come and die. Bonhoeffer took this literally—he was eventually executed by the Nazis for his role in the political resistance movement. God's grace should mean something, he argued, and it should bring about justice on earth. "Cheap grace is the deadly enemy of our Church," he wrote. "We are fighting today for costly grace."

It can be said that Clinton knows this personally all too well. Few people in politics today know costs as closely as she does, be they political, marital, or the costs of being the first woman poised to become president. They have followed her time and again throughout her career. But she keeps on going. As she told a gathering of Methodist women in April, "Even when the odds are long, even when we are tired and just want to go away somewhere to be alone and rest, let's make it happen."

In a way, the costs are just the price for doing the Lord's work. And it makes politics, and whatever her future therein is, more than just her career: it makes it her calling.

HOLDING ONTO FAITH
*The Clintons (in 2001)
attended Foundry United
Methodist Church in
Washington, D.C.*

THE FAMILY BUSINESS

AS PARTNERS IN HILLARY'S POLITICAL
DYNASTY, BILL AND CHELSEA BRING A LOT TO
THE PARTY, AS WELL AS SOME BAGGAGE
BY HALEY SWEETLAND EDWARDS

BACKING HER RUN
*Presidential candidate
Hillary gets high-wattage
help from Bill and Chelsea
at a 2007 New York rally.*

W

When Chelsea Clinton announced in April 2014 that she was pregnant, it took the media about two nanoseconds to zero in on what that could mean for national politics. Namely, that Hillary, should she run for president in 2016, could campaign as a grandmother. Within hours, Democratic analysts predicted gleefully that the new role could be a "game changer" on the campaign trail, while Republicans downplayed the potential shift in public persona. A few of the more conservative commentators even suggested, rudely, that the Clintons had planned the pregnancy to maximize good optics in 2016. The morning after the announcement, *New York Times* columnist Andrew Ross Sorkin, on MSNBC's *Morning Joe*, described the disclosure as the beginning of "the human drama that is Grandma Clinton."

The speculation, while admittedly absurd—calculating the political implications of an unborn child requires a certain audacity, at least—was also an indication,

as Sorkin suggested, of the continuing role that the Clinton family has played in the American political drama for a generation. The Clintons have been more or less constantly on stage since the late '70s, when Bill first ran for governor of Arkansas. After Clinton entered the White House in 1993, Chelsea was featured in 87 network news stories and 32 articles in the *New York Times*, among the most of any president's kid, according to the political scientist Robert Watson. And the White House years were just another act in the long-running drama. We have, over the years, carefully scrutinized their decisions, their health scares, their haircuts; we have weighed in on their missteps and victories. We were there when Bill joined the ex-presidents club and when Chelsea went to high school, then college, then graduate school. We had front-row seats when Hillary's political star began to rise, first as a U.S. senator from New York and then as the secretary of state. And we watched as the Clinton Global Initiative (CGI) and the recently renamed Bill, Hillary & Chelsea Clinton Family Foundation became one of the most influential players in the field of international development.

The question now is whether all that history—a quarter-century of memories, goodwill and baggage—will help or hurt if Hillary runs for president in 2016. Voters tend to like political dynasties in both parties, almost despite those dynasties' history. America is on its fourth generation of Bushes; Mitt Romney's father ran for

VICTORS' WALK *The First Lady (with the outgoing president and Chelsea in Nov. 2000) won her New York Senate seat with 55% of the vote.*

FATHER OF THE BRIDE *Bill walks Chelsea down the aisle in Rhinebeck, N.Y., in July 2010.*

president in 1968, 40 years before the son mounted his first run. Al Gore's father was in national politics long before his son tried his hand. Even Rand Paul is a legatee of his libertarian father's years in Congress. The ways that candidates with familiar names both fit in with and stand apart from their clans matter, because such behavior is a window into their values, priorities and private lives.

The good news for Clinton supporters is that, according to an April 2014 *Washington Post*/ABC News poll, 66% of Americans viewed the Clinton family favorably. Analysts say that's largely because many Americans remember the Clinton era, from 1993 to 2001, as one in which the economy was booming, unemployment was down, wars were won quickly, and important federal issues, like welfare reform, were

actually addressed head-on. Bill Clinton's charisma and charm is a trickier thing to measure: like it or not, he has an almost preternatural ability to connect with voters young and old, black and white, rich and poor. But if he was at times Hillary's secret weapon in 2008—acting as headliner at fundraisers, expert interview-giver, proxy and consultant—his feel for the electorate was sometimes off-target.

Chelsea, for her part, has dutifully campaigned for both her parents over the years. Chelsea remembers, as she told *Fast Company* magazine in May 2014, waving little American flags at her father's gubernatorial races in the early '80s, when she was barely 3. More recently, on her mother's primary-campaign trail in 2008, Chelsea gave hundreds of speeches, mostly on college campuses, where she—herself a bright-eyed,

articulate member of the millennial generation—worked to connect with young people,
a demographic to whom her then-60-year-
old mother had a harder time appealing.

If Hillary throws her hat in the ring in
2016, analysts expect that both husband
and daughter will play larger, and perhaps
better-defined, roles in the next campaign.
Bill, whose speech at the 2012 Democratic
National Convention electrified the audience and sent pundits writing encomiums
about Bill as the "greatest communicator,"
will likely be used to win over key voting
groups and pull in influential help, while
Chelsea is expected to take on a fairly
robust high-level role, possibly in strategic
management. "I can see her being a senior
adviser," Amie Parnes, co-author of the
recent *New York Times* best seller *HRC: State
Secrets and the Rebirth of Hillary Clinton*, told
Fast Company.

Regardless of what happens next, the
Clintons' center of gravity as of now is CGI
and the Clinton Family Foundation, which
together employ more than 2,000 people
in 36 countries. CGI has helped create $103
billion of pledges to 2,800 philanthropic
projects around the globe. Unlike other
family-branded foundations like the Gates
Foundation, which disburse families'
personal wealth, Bill, Hillary and Chelsea
must solicit grants from wealthy friends
and corporations to fund projects that
range from curbing global warming to ending elephant poaching. In 2014 the foundation launched the "No Ceilings" project,
which Chelsea will help steer and which
will monitor and facilitate the progress of
women and girls worldwide.

The financial motor behind much of
these efforts is CGI, which hosts an annual
conference in Manhattan and draws the
brightest stars from the political and development firmament, each of whom coughs
up a $20,000 yearly membership fee to cozy

up with one another for the three-day love-
fest. For campaign-finance and tax reasons,
no dollars raised by CGI or the Clinton
Family Foundation can be used toward Hillary's—or anyone else's—campaign, although
the relationships developed beneath the CGI
umbrella are, of course, fair game. Both critics and admirers of the Clintons have noted
that the family's charity work has allowed
them to assemble a team of wealthy donors,
while simultaneously cultivating a reputation for service, a position that certainly
doesn't hurt a national campaign. It also
offers Chelsea, who recently started working at the foundation ("I joined the family
business," as she puts it), the opportunity to
work closely with her mother in an organi-
zational capacity, should she end up taking
on a similar position in her campaign.

"You can see it already," Parnes said in
Fast Company. "She and her mom are working on these issues together ... Something
her mom learned last time was that there
was arrogance at the top. She wasn't hearing the truth from people, and Chelsea will
give her the truth."

But while in this context the Clintons
may appear an unstoppable triumvirate,
their arms around each other's waists at
state dinners, funerals, fundraisers, galas
and countless charity events, the media—
and their rivals—have hardly forgotten their
less-TV-ready past. In an interview with
Vanity Fair in April, Monica Lewinsky herself came forward to defend Hillary, asking
the nation to "bury the blue dress," while
Senator Rand Paul, whose name is floated
as a potential nominee in 2016, has done
everything he can to resurrect it. In an interview with *Meet the Press* in late Jan. 2014,
the Kentucky Republican suggested that the
Clinton family's social advocacy, especially
with regard to girls' and women's rights, is
disingenuous, given what he described as
Bill's "predatory behavior" toward women

CAPE COD RESPITE
Hillary, Chelsea and Bill relax for a portrait in 1993 on Martha's Vineyard, a favorite getaway.

while he was in office. "If they want to take [a] position on women's rights, by all means do," he said in early February on C-Span. "But you can't do it and take it from a guy who was using his position of authority to take advantage of young women in the workplace." Paul's wife, Kelley Ashby, also suggested in a *Vogue* article in 2013 that Bill's history with Monica Lewinsky "should complicate his return to the White House, even as First Spouse."

And well it may. But trying to make an issue of the Clinton family's well-litigated past could also backfire during a time in this country when unemployment is still high, real wages are declining, and Americans are feeling squeezed. The electorate may feel that attacking Hillary for the mistakes of her husband (for which she has already paid a painful price) is simply untoward. Nor does it follow that the past is prologue. In the late '90s, the Clinton family is arguably what helped refurbish Bill's legacy. Following a press conference in 1998 in which the president admitted that he had had an affair, Chelsea, who was 18 years old, walked between her mother and father and held each of their hands. The resulting image—the visual equivalent of sticking-togetherness, of forgiveness—came to define the Clintons in the following year.

As for Hillary's future role as grandmother? To indulge in a bit of our own speculation: the precious bundle could be a mixed blessing, in political terms. The most obvious risk to Hillary's new role is that it will inevitably highlight her age, a vulnerability some conservatives have already begun exploiting. (At 66, Hillary is "not particularly old for a man," conservative columnist Wes Pruden argued last year, but "a woman in public life is getting past her sell-by date.") And although such calculations might rightly infuriate feminists—who cared how many grandchildren Mitt

Romney had?—whether Hillary is being a "good grandma" or not may make headlines as well.

By the same token, however, becoming a grandmother could also help Hillary excite and relate to younger voters for whom the title of "grandmother" is powerful. While it might have been a political liability in 1975 to be seen as a graying older lady, the role has taken on new meaning, particularly among younger, black and Latino voters, whose families are often bound by strong matriarchs. "In a world where nearly 40% of new mothers are single, many communities rely on grandmothers to hold together the whole family," says Anne Liston, a Democratic strategist. "The image of a grandmother is one of a compassionate caregiver."

That might be exactly the ace in the hole that Hillary needs as a national candidate. While poll after poll has found that voters find her competent, strong, intelligent and electable, in 2008 she struggled to connect with crowds of even strongly Democratic supporters, who found her calculating or aloof. Becoming a grandmother could help her warm up her public image and provide her speechwriters with a supply of rich material that they could use to connect her to the advocacy for children, families and public health that she's championed for decades.

Of course, regardless of how deftly Hillary fits into her new role, and no matter how solid the Clinton family is, her many critics will complain. They will, as they have before, remind voters of past mistakes or paint Chelsea as a pawn of her parents' political regime. They'll accuse Hillary of using the grandchild as a campaign tool and suggest that the Clintons' considerable influence is misused. But throughout it all, the Clintons will have one another, holding hands onstage. And if the past 25 years is any indication, it can be unwise to underestimate their staying power.

BUSMAN'S HOLIDAY
The Clintons enjoy a Yellowstone sunset on Aug. 12, 1996, the day Bill outlawed mining in the park.

TIME

Managing Editor Nancy Gibbs
Creative Director D.W. Pine
Director of Photography Kira Pollack

HILLARY: AN AMERICAN LIFE

Editors Stephen Koepp, Michael Duffy
Designer Chrissy Dunleavy
Photo Editor Crary Pullen
Contributors Alex Altman, Massimo Calabresi, Michael Crowley, Elizabeth Dias, Zeke Miller, Jay Newton-Small, Michael Scherer, Haley Sweetland Edwards, David Von Drehle
Researchers Melissa August, Mary Alice Shaughnessy
Editorial Production David Sloan

Time Home Entertainment

Publisher Jim Childs
Executive Director, Marketing Services Carol Pittard
Executive Director, Retail & Special Sales Tom Mifsud
Executive Publishing Director Joy Bomba
Director, Bookazine Development & Marketing Laura Adam
Vice President, Finance Vandana Patel
Publishing Director Megan Pearlman
Assistant General Counsel Simone Procas
Assistant Director, Special Sales Ilene Schreider
Brand Manager Bryan Christian
Associate Production Manager Kimberly Marshall
Associate Prepress Manager Alex Voznesenskiy

Editorial Director Stephen Koepp
Senior Editor Roe D'Angelo
Copy Chief Rina Bander
Design Manager Anne-Michelle Gallero
Editorial Operations Gina Scauzillo

Special thanks Katherine Barnet, Brad Beatson, Jeremy Biloon, Susan Chodakiewicz, Rose Cirrincione, Assu Etsubneh, Mariana Evans, Christine Font, Susan Hettleman, Hillary Hirsch, David Kahn, Jean Kennedy, Daniel S. Levy, Amy Mangus, Nina Mistry, David Olivenbaum, Dave Rozzelle, Ricardo Santiago, Holly Smith, Adriana Tierno, Time Inc. Premedia

ISBN 10: 1-61893-118-0; ISBN 13: 978-1-61893-118-4
Library of Congress Control Number: 2014937116
We welcome your comments and suggestions about TIME Books. Please write to us at: TIME Books, Attention: Book Editors, P.O. Box 11016, Des Moines, IA 50336-1016
If you would like to order any of our hardcover Collector's Edition books, please call us at 800-327-6388, Monday through Friday, 7 a.m.–8 p.m., or Saturday, 7 a.m.–6 p.m., Central Time.

'ARE YOU READY FOR CHANGE?' *Hillary asked Iowa voters on Jan. 1, 2008, two days before the state caucus vote.*

COVER
Marco Grob/Trunk Archive for TIME

BACK COVER
Aaron R. Cohen/Corbis

ENDPAPERS
Lee Balterman/Time & Life Pictures

TITLE PAGE
1 Stan Honda/AFP/Getty Images

CONTENTS
2-3 Elsie Amendola/AP

INTRODUCTION
4-5 Jacquelyn Martin/Pool/AP;
7 Olivier Douliery/Abacausa.com

NEXT RUN
8-9 Douglas Friedman/Trunk Archive;
11 Yuri Gripas/Reuters; 12 Nicholas
Kamm/AFP/Getty Images; 13 Mary F.
Calvert for the Washington Post/Getty
Images; 15 Gerald Herbert/AP;
17 Patsy Lynch/Retna/Corbis;
19 Jonathan Ernst/Reuters/Corbis

BY THE NUMBERS
21 (from top) Richard Ellis/Getty
Images; Getty Images; Chuck Kennedy/
MCT/Getty Images

EARLY YEARS
23 Sygma/Corbis; 25 Polaris (4);
27 Sygma/Corbis; 28 Polaris;
31-37 Mike Stewart/Sygma/Corbis

WHITE HOUSE
38-39 Jeffrey Markowitz/Sygma/
Corbis; 41 © Yousuf Karsh; 42
Wally McNamee/Corbis; 43 Jeffrey
Markowitz/Sygma/Corbis; 44 Atlas
Archive/The Image Works; 46 Win
McNamee/Reuters; 47 Richard Ellis/
Zuma Press; 48-49 Jean-Louis Atlan/
Paris Match/Getty Images; 50 Dirck
Halstead/Getty Images; 51 Susan
Walsh/AP; 52-53 Harry Hamburg/
New York Daily News/Getty Images

SENATE
54-55 Photo illustration by Albert
Watson; 57 Shawn Thew/Gamma;
58 Dusan Vranic/Reuters; 60-61 Kevin
Lamarque/Reuters; 63 David Scull/
Gamma

FIRST BID
64-65 Christopher Morris/VII for
TIME; 66-67 Charles Dharapak/AP;
68 Paul Sancya/AP; 70-71 David
Burnett/Contact Press Images;
73 Christopher Morris/VII for TIME;
74-75 Chuck Kennedy/MCT/
Getty Images

STATE DEPARTMENT
76-77 Christopher Anderson/Magnum
Photos; 78-79 Pete Souza/The White
House; 80 Mikhail Metzel/AFP/Getty
Images; 81-83 Brendan Smialowski/
Pool/AP; 84 Chuck Kennedy/The White
House; 87 Andrew Harrer/Bloomberg/
Getty Images; 88 Brendan Smialowski/
Pool/AP

TIME COVERS
90-91 Top row, from left: Gregory
Heisler, Steve Liss, Dirck Halstead,
Brad Markel/Gamma, photomontage
by Arthur Hochstein, Albert Watson,
second row, from left: Blake Sell/
Reuters, photomontage by Arthur
Hochstein, Aaron Shikler, Patrick
Demarchelier, photo illustration by
John Ritter, photograph by Brooks
Kraft; photomontage with photographs
by Callie Shell (Obama) and Damon
Winter (Clinton); third row, from left:
photomontage with photographs by
Diana Walker (Clinton) and Doug Mills
(Obama), David Burnett, Diana Walker,
Marco Grob, Diana Walker, photo
illustration by Justin Metz; all courtesy
of Time Inc.

FAITH
92-93 Brooks Kraft/Corbis for TIME;
95 Mike Stewart/Sygma/Corbis;
96 Sylwia Kapuscinski/The New York
Times/Redux; 99 Shawn Thew/Gamma

FAMILY
100-101 Keith Bedford/Reuters/
Corbis; 103 Khue Bui; 104 Genevieve
de Manio; 106-107 Alfred Eisenstaedt/
Time & Life Pictures/Getty Images;
109 Paul J. Richards/AFP/Getty Images

MASTHEAD AND CREDITS
110-111 Doug Mills/The New York
Times/Redux; 112 Stan Honda/AFP/
Getty Images

IS IT HER TIME? *While Clinton insists she hasn't decided, the polls and pundits predict that Americans would elect another history-making president.*